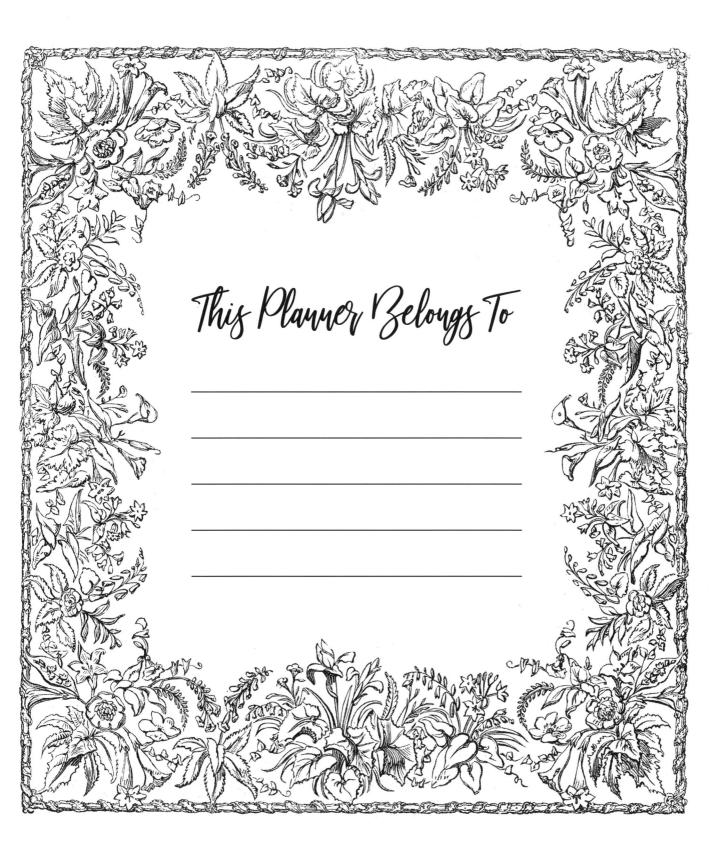

This Planner Belongs To

_____

_____

_____

_____

_____

Create Your January Budget Here

MONTHLY INCOMES

#	SOURCE	AMOUNT	DATE
1.		$	
2.		$	
3.		$	
4.		$	
5.		$	

TOTAL INCOME: $ _____

Wealth consists not in having great possessions, but in having few wants.
–Epictetus

MONTHLY EXPENSES
UTILITIES

RENT / MORTGAGE--------- $ _____
ELECTRICITY BILL--------- $ _____
WATER BILL------------ $ _____
SEWAGE / TRASH-------- $ _____
CABLE BILL----------- $ _____
INTERNET---------- $ _____
PHONE BILL(S)-------- $ _____

TOTAL UTILITIES: $ _____

MONTHLY EXPENSES
HEALTHCARE

HEALTH INSURANCE--------- $ _____
LIFE INSURANCE---------- $ _____
DENTAL INSURANCE------- $ _____
DOCTOR APPOINTMENT(S)- $ _____
DENTAL APPOINTMENT(S)- $ _____
OPTOMETRY APPOINTMENT(S)- $ _____
PERSCRIPTIONS---------- $ _____
OTHER MEDICAL EXPENSES--- $ _____

TOTAL HEALTHCARE: $ _____

LIVING EXPENSES

GROCERIES----------- $ _____
BEAUTY SUPPLIES-------- $ _____
BEAUTY APPOINTMENTS---- $ _____
MEMBERSHIP DUES / FEES-- $ _____
DAYCARE / BABYSITTER ---- $ _____
School SUPPLIES---------- $ _____
SCHOOL CLUB(S) DUES / FEES-- $ _____
NEW CLOTHING---------- $ _____
ALLOWANCES---------- $ _____
OTHER LIVING EXPENSES---- $ _____

TOTAL LIVING EXPENSES: $ _____

MONTHLY EXPENSES

PET EXPENSES

PET INSURANCE-------------- $_____
PET FOOD------------------- $_____
VETERINARY APPOINTMENT(S)--- $_____
NEW TOYS / TREATS---------- $_____
PET SITTER / DAYCARE------- $_____
OTHER PET EXPENSES--------- $_____

TOTAL PET EXPENSES: $_____

TRANSPORTATION

AUTOMOBILE INSURANCE------ $_____
AUTOMOBILE PAYMENTS------- $_____
MONTHLY FUEL COSTS-------- $_____
REPAIRS / MAINTENANCE----- $_____
FARES / TICKETS /ETC.----- $_____
OTHER TRANSPORTATION EXPENSES-- $_____

TOTAL TRANSPORTATION: $_____

GIFT EXPENSES

MONTHLY BIRTHDAYS---------- $_____
MONTHLY HOLIDAYS---------- $_____
OTHER GIFT EXPENSES------- $_____

TOTAL GIFT EXPENSES: $_____

MONTHLY EXPENSES

HOUSING EXPENSES

RENTER'S / HOMEOWNER'S INSURANCE--- $_____
CLEANING SUPPLIES--------- $_____
GARDENING SUPPLIES-------- $_____
FURNISHINGS--------------- $_____
LAUNDRY / DRY CLEANING- $_____
HOME MAINTENANCE / REPAIRS-- $_____
HOUSEHOLD NECESSITIES---- $_____
OTHER HOUSING EXPENSES--- $_____

TOTAL HOUSING EXPENSES: $_____

RECREATION

VACATION(S)--------------- $_____
DINING OUT--------------- $_____
ENTERTAINMENT------------ $_____
SOCIAL EVENTS----------- $_____
OTHER RECREATION EXPENESES--- $_____

TOTAL RECREATION EXPENSES: $_____

SAVINGS

EMERGENCY FUND----------- $_____
EDUCATION FUND---------- $_____
RETIREMENT FUND--------- $_____

TOTAL SAVINGS: $_____

_January_____

MONTHLY EXPENSES

DEBTS

CREDIT CARD #1 ----------- $____
CREDIT CARD #2 ----------- $____
CREDIT CARD #3 ----------- $____
CREDIT CARD #4 ----------- $____
PRIVATE DEBTS ----------- $____
OTHER DEBTS ----------- $____

TOTAL DEBTS: $_____

OTHER EXPENSES

OTHER EXPENSE #1 --------- $____
OTHER EXPENSE #2 --------- $____
OTHER EXPENSE #3 --------- $____

TOTAL OTHER EXPENSES: $_____

MONTHLY BUDGET

TOTAL INCOME: $_____
— TOTAL EXPENSES: $_____

MONEY REMAINING: $_____

MONTHLY NOTES

January

MONTHLY BILL TRACKING

PAID	BILL NAME	DUE DATE	AMOUNT DUE	AMOUNT PAID	BALANCE	PAYMENT METHOD / NOTES
○						
○						
○						
○						
○						
○						
○						
○						
○						
○						
○						
○						
○						
○						
○						
○						
○						
○						
○						
○						
○						
○						
○						
○						
○						
○						
○						

Create Your February Budget Here

MONTHLY INCOMES

#	SOURCE	AMOUNT	DATE
1.		$	
2.		$	
3.		$	
4.		$	
5.		$	

TOTAL INCOME: $____

Money often costs too much.
-Ralph Waldo Emerson

MONTHLY EXPENSES
UTILITIES

RENT / MORTGAGE---------- $____
ELECTRICITY BILL---------- $____
WATER BILL------------ $____
SEWAGE / TRASH--------- $____
CABLE BILL------------ $____
INTERNET------------- $____
PHONE BILL(S)---------- $____

TOTAL UTILITIES: $____

MONTHLY EXPENSES
HEALTHCARE

HEALTH INSURANCE---------- $____
LIFE INSURANCE---------- $____
DENTAL INSURANCE------- $____
DOCTOR APPOINTMENT(S)-$____
DENTAL APPOINTMENT(S)-$____
OPTOMETRY APPOINTMENT(S)-$____
PERSCRIPTIONS---------- $____
OTHER MEDICAL EXPENSES--- $____

TOTAL HEALTHCARE: $____

LIVING EXPENSES

GROCERIES------------ $____
BEAUTY SUPPLIES--------- $____
BEAUTY APPOINTMENTS---- $____
MEMBERSHIP DUES / FEES-- $____
DAYCARE / BABYSITTER ---- $____
School SUPPLIES--------- $____
SCHOOL CLUB(S) DUES / FEES-- $____
NEW CLOTHING---------- $____
ALLOWANCES----------- $____
OTHER LIVING EXPENSES---- $____

TOTAL LIVING EXPENSES: $____

MONTHLY EXPENSES

PET EXPENSES

PET INSURANCE----------- $_____
PET FOOD----------------- $_____
VETERINARY APPOINTMENT(S)-- $_____
NEW TOYS / TREATS ------- $_____
PET SITTER / DAYCARE----- $_____
OTHER PET EXPENSES------- $_____

TOTAL PET EXPENSES: $_____

TRANSPORTATION

AUTOMOBILE INSURANCE---- $_____
AUTOMOBILE PAYMENTS--- $_____
MONTHLY FUEL COSTS------ $_____
REPAIRS / MAINTENANCE-- $_____
FARES / TICKETS / ETC.----- $_____
OTHER TRANSPORTATION EXPENSES-- $_____

TOTAL TRANSPORTATION: $_____

GIFT EXPENSES

MONTHLY BIRTHDAYS--------- $_____
MONTHLY HOLIDAYS------- $_____
OTHER GIFT EXPENSES------- $_____

TOTAL GIFT EXPENSES: $_____

MONTHLY EXPENSES

HOUSING EXPENSES

RENTER'S / HOMEOWNER'S INSURANCE--- $_____
CLEANING SUPPLIES------- $_____
GARDENING SUPPLIES------- $_____
FURNISHINGS----------- $_____
LAUNDRY / DRY CLEANING- $_____
HOME MAINTENANCE / REPAIRS-- $_____
HOUSEHOLD NECESSITIES---- $_____
OTHER HOUSING EXPENSES--- $_____

TOTAL HOUSING EXPENSES: $_____

RECREATION

VACATION(S)----------- $_____
DINING OUT----------- $_____
ENTERTAINMENT--------- $_____
SOCIAL EVENTS--------- $_____
OTHER RECREATION EXPENESES--- $_____

TOTAL RECREATION EXPENSES: $_____

SAVINGS

EMERGENCY FUND----------- $_____
EDUCATION FUND------- $_____
RETIREMENT FUND--------- $_____

TOTAL SAVINGS: $_____

February _____

MONTHLY EXPENSES

DEBTS

CREDIT CARD #1 ----------- $ _____
CREDIT CARD #2 ----------- $ _____
CREDIT CARD #3 ----------- $ _____
CREDIT CARD #4 ----------- $ _____
PRIVATE DEBTS ----------- $ _____
OTHER DEBTS ----------- $ _____

TOTAL DEBTS: $ _____

OTHER EXPENSES

OTHER EXPENSE #1 ----------- $ _____
OTHER EXPENSE #2 ----------- $ _____
OTHER EXPENSE #3 ----------- $ _____

TOTAL OTHER EXPENSES: $ _____

MONTHLY BUDGET

TOTAL INCOME: $ _____
— TOTAL EXPENSES: $ _____

MONEY REMAINING: $ _____

MONTHLY NOTES

February

MONTHLY BILL TRACKING

PAID	BILL NAME	DUE DATE	AMOUNT DUE	AMOUNT PAID	BALANCE	PAYMENT METHOD / NOTES
○						
○						
○						
○						
○						
○						
○						
○						
○						
○						
○						
○						
○						
○						
○						
○						
○						
○						
○						
○						
○						
○						
○						
○						
○						
○						
○						

Create Your March Budget Here

MONTHLY INCOMES

#	SOURCE	AMOUNT	DATE
1.		$	
2.		$	
3.		$	
4.		$	
5.		$	

TOTAL INCOME: $ _____

An investment in knowledge pays the best interest.
-Benjamin Franklin

MONTHLY EXPENSES
UTILITIES

RENT / MORTGAGE---------$_____
ELECTRICITY BILL---------$_____
WATER BILL-----------$_____
SEWAGE / TRASH--------$_____
CABLE BILL-----------$_____
INTERNET-----------$_____
PHONE BILL(S)---------$_____

TOTAL UTILITIES: $_____

MONTHLY EXPENSES
HEALTHCARE

HEALTH INSURANCE----------$_____
LIFE INSURANCE----------$_____
DENTAL INSURANCE--------$_____
DOCTOR APPOINTMENT(S)-$_____
DENTAL APPOINTMENT(S)-$_____
OPTOMETRY APPOINTMENT(S)-$_____
PERSCRIPTIONS----------$_____
OTHER MEDICAL EXPENSES---$_____

TOTAL HEALTHCARE: $_____

LIVING EXPENSES

GROCERIES-----------$_____
BEAUTY SUPPLIES--------$_____
BEAUTY APPOINTMENTS----$_____
MEMBERSHIP DUES / FEES--$_____
DAYCARE / BABYSITTER----$_____
SCHOOL SUPPLIES---------$_____
SCHOOL CLUB(S) DUES / FEES--$_____
NEW CLOTHING---------$_____
ALLOWANCES----------$_____
OTHER LIVING EXPENSES----$_____

TOTAL LIVING EXPENSES: $_____

MONTHLY EXPENSES

PET EXPENSES

PET INSURANCE----------------- $ ____
PET FOOD---------------------- $ ____
VETERINARY APPOINTMENT(s)--- $ ____
New toys / treats ----------- $ ____
Pet sitter / daycare------- $ ____
OTHER PET EXPENSES-------- $ ____

TOTAL PET EXPENSES: $ ____

TRANSPORTATION

AUTOMOBILE INSURANCE----- $ ____
AUTOMOBILE PAYMENTS---- $ ____
MONTHLY FUEL COSTS------- $ ____
REPAIRS / MAINTENANCE--- $ ____
FARES / TICKETS / ETC.----- $ ____
OTHER TRANSPORTATION EXPENSES-- $ ____

TOTAL TRANSPORTATION: $ ____

GIFT EXPENSES

Monthly Birthdays---------- $ ____
MONTHLY HOLIDAYS------- $ ____
OTHER GIFT EXPENSES------- $ ____

TOTAL GIFT EXPENSES: $ ____

MONTHLY EXPENSES

HOUSING EXPENSES

RENTER'S / HOMEOWNER'S INSURANCE--- $ ____
CLEANING SUPPLIES------- $ ____
GARDENING SUPPLIES------- $ ____
FURNISHINGS------------- $ ____
LAUNDRY / DRY CLEANING- $ ____
HOME MAINTENANCE / REPAIRS-- $ ____
HOUSEHOLD NECESSITIES---- $ ____
OTHER HOUSING EXPENSES--- $ ____

TOTAL HOUSING EXPENSES: $ ____

RECREATION

VACATION(s)------------- $ ____
DINING OUT------------- $ ____
ENTERTAINMENT--------- $ ____
SOCIAL EVENTS--------- $ ____
OTHER RECREATION EXPENESES--- $ ____

TOTAL RECREATION EXPENSES: $ ____

SAVINGS

EMERGENCY FUND------------ $ ____
EDUCATION FUND-------- $ ____
RETIREMENT FUND-------- $ ____

TOTAL SAVINGS: $ ____

March _____

MONTHLY EXPENSES

DEBTS

CREDIT CARD #1 -------------- $ _____
CREDIT CARD #2 -------------- $ _____
CREDIT CARD #3 -------------- $ _____
CREDIT CARD #4 -------------- $ _____
PRIVATE DEBTS --------- $ _____
OTHER DEBTS --------- $ _____

TOTAL DEBTS: $ _____

OTHER EXPENSES

OTHER EXPENSE #1 --------- $ _____
OTHER EXPENSE #2 --------- $ _____
OTHER EXPENSE #3 --------- $ _____

TOTAL OTHER EXPENSES: $ _____

MONTHLY BUDGET

TOTAL INCOME: $ _____
— TOTAL EXPENSES: $ _____

MONEY REMAINING: $ _____

MONTHLY NOTES

_____
_____
_____
_____
_____
_____
_____
_____
_____
_____
_____
_____
_____
_____
_____
_____
_____
_____
_____
_____
_____
_____
_____
_____
_____
_____
_____
_____
_____

MONTHLY BILL TRACKING

March_____

PAID	BILL NAME	DUE DATE	AMOUNT DUE	AMOUNT PAID	BALANCE	PAYMENT METHOD / NOTES
○						
○						
○						
○						
○						
○						
○						
○						
○						
○						
○						
○						
○						
○						
○						
○						
○						
○						
○						
○						
○						
○						
○						
○						
○						

Create Your April Budget Here

MONTHLY INCOMES

#	SOURCE	AMOUNT	DATE
1.		$	
2.		$	
3.		$	
4.		$	
5.		$	

TOTAL INCOME: $_____

> Opportunity is missed by most people because it is dressed in overalls and looks like work.
> —Thomas Edison

MONTHLY EXPENSES
UTILITIES

RENT / MORTGAGE --------- $_____
ELECTRICITY BILL --------- $_____
WATER BILL ------------- $_____
SEWAGE / TRASH --------- $_____
CABLE BILL ------------- $_____
INTERNET -------------- $_____
PHONE BILL(S) ---------- $_____

TOTAL UTILITIES: $_____

MONTHLY EXPENSES
HEALTHCARE

HEALTH INSURANCE --------- $_____
LIFE INSURANCE ---------- $_____
DENTAL INSURANCE -------- $_____
DOCTOR APPOINTMENT(S) - $_____
DENTAL APPOINTMENT(S) - $_____
OPTOMETRY APPOINTMENT(S) - $_____
PERSCRIPTIONS ---------- $_____
OTHER MEDICAL EXPENSES --- $_____

TOTAL HEALTHCARE: $_____

LIVING EXPENSES

GROCERIES -------------- $_____
BEAUTY SUPPLIES --------- $_____
BEAUTY APPOINTMENTS ---- $_____
MEMBERSHIP DUES / FEES -- $_____
DAYCARE / BABYSITTER ---- $_____
SCHOOL SUPPLIES --------- $_____
SCHOOL CLUB(S) DUES / FEES -- $_____
NEW CLOTHING ---------- $_____
ALLOWANCES ------------ $_____
OTHER LIVING EXPENSES ---- $_____

TOTAL LIVING EXPENSES: $_____

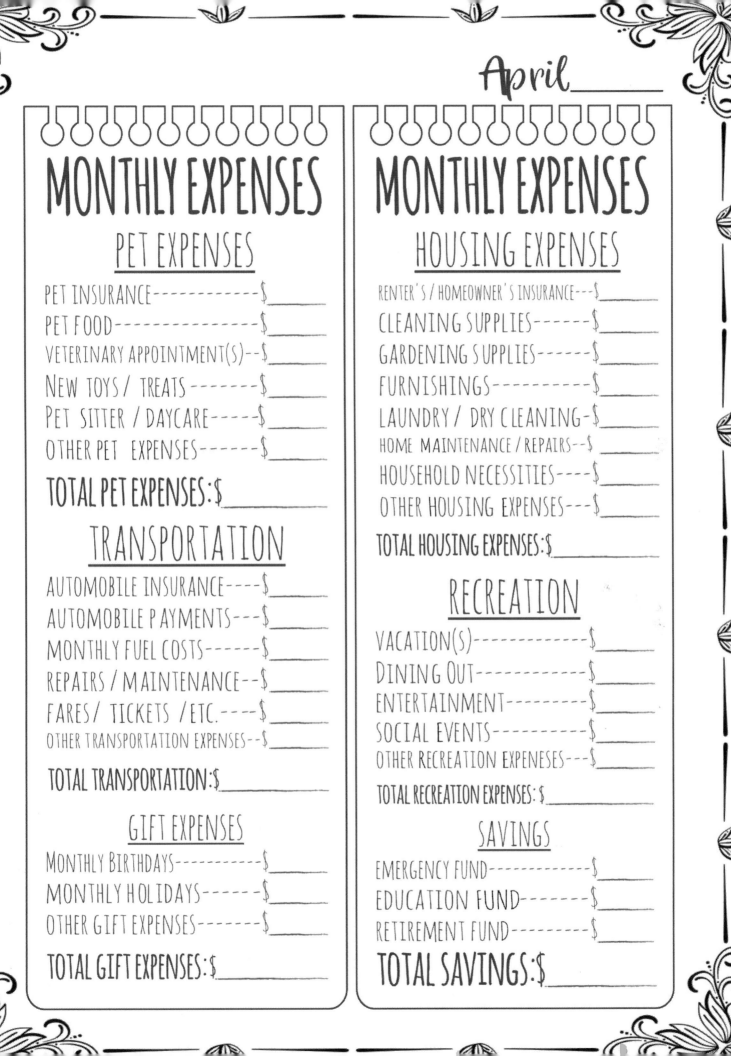

April_____

MONTHLY EXPENSES
PET EXPENSES

PET INSURANCE----------$_____
PET FOOD--------------$_____
VETERINARY APPOINTMENT(S)--$_____
NEW TOYS / TREATS------$_____
PET SITTER / DAYCARE-----$_____
OTHER PET EXPENSES------$_____

TOTAL PET EXPENSES:$_____

TRANSPORTATION

AUTOMOBILE INSURANCE----$_____
AUTOMOBILE PAYMENTS---$_____
MONTHLY FUEL COSTS------$_____
REPAIRS / MAINTENANCE--$_____
FARES / TICKETS /ETC.----$_____
OTHER TRANSPORTATION EXPENSES--$_____

TOTAL TRANSPORTATION:$_____

GIFT EXPENSES

MONTHLY BIRTHDAYS---------$_____
MONTHLY HOLIDAYS------$_____
OTHER GIFT EXPENSES-------$_____

TOTAL GIFT EXPENSES:$_____

MONTHLY EXPENSES
HOUSING EXPENSES

RENTER'S / HOMEOWNER'S INSURANCE---$_____
CLEANING SUPPLIES------$_____
GARDENING SUPPLIES------$_____
FURNISHINGS-----------$_____
LAUNDRY / DRY CLEANING-$_____
HOME MAINTENANCE / REPAIRS--$_____
HOUSEHOLD NECESSITIES----$_____
OTHER HOUSING EXPENSES---$_____

TOTAL HOUSING EXPENSES:$_____

RECREATION

VACATION(S)-----------$_____
DINING OUT-----------$_____
ENTERTAINMENT--------$_____
SOCIAL EVENTS--------$_____
OTHER RECREATION EXPENSES---$_____

TOTAL RECREATION EXPENSES: $_____

SAVINGS

EMERGENCY FUND---------$_____
EDUCATION FUND-------$_____
RETIREMENT FUND-------$_____

TOTAL SAVINGS:$_____

April_____

MONTHLY EXPENSES

DEBTS

CREDIT CARD #1 ----------- $_____
CREDIT CARD #2 ----------- $_____
CREDIT CARD #3 ----------- $_____
CREDIT CARD #4 ----------- $_____
PRIVATE DEBTS ---------- $_____
OTHER DEBTS ----------- $_____

TOTAL DEBTS: $_____

OTHER EXPENSES

OTHER EXPENSE #1 --------- $_____
OTHER EXPENSE #2 --------- $_____
OTHER EXPENSE #3 --------- $_____

TOTAL OTHER EXPENSES: $_____

MONTHLY BUDGET

TOTAL INCOME: $_____
− TOTAL EXPENSES: $_____
_____

MONEY REMAINING: $_____

MONTHLY NOTES

_____
_____
_____
_____
_____
_____
_____
_____
_____
_____
_____
_____
_____
_____
_____
_____
_____
_____
_____
_____
_____
_____
_____
_____
_____
_____
_____
_____

MONTHLY BILL TRACKING

April _____

PAID	BILL NAME	DUE DATE	AMOUNT DUE	AMOUNT PAID	BALANCE	PAYMENT METHOD / NOTES
○						
○						
○						
○						
○						
○						
○						
○						
○						
○						
○						
○						
○						
○						
○						
○						
○						
○						
○						
○						
○						
○						
○						
○						
○						
○						
○						
○						

Create Your May Budget Here

MONTHLY INCOMES

#	SOURCE	AMOUNT	DATE
1.		$	
2.		$	
3.		$	
4.		$	
5.		$	

TOTAL INCOME: $ _____

It is not the man who has too little, but the man who craves more, that is poor.
—Seneca

MONTHLY EXPENSES

UTILITIES

RENT / MORTGAGE --------- $ _____
ELECTRICITY BILL --------- $ _____
WATER BILL --------- $ _____
SEWAGE / TRASH --------- $ _____
CABLE BILL --------- $ _____
INTERNET --------- $ _____
Phone Bill(s) --------- $ _____

TOTAL UTILITIES: $ _____

MONTHLY EXPENSES

HEALTHCARE

HEALTH INSURANCE --------- $ _____
LIFE INSURANCE --------- $ _____
DENTAL INSURANCE --------- $ _____
DOCTOR APPOINTMENT(S) - $ _____
DENTAL APPOINTMENT(S) - $ _____
OPTOMETRY APPOINTMENT(S) - $ _____
PERSCRIPTIONS --------- $ _____
OTHER MEDICAL EXPENSES --- $ _____

TOTAL HEALTHCARE: $ _____

LIVING EXPENSES

GROCERIES --------- $ _____
BEAUTY SUPPLIES --------- $ _____
BEAUTY APPOINTMENTS --- $ _____
MEMBERSHIP DUES / FEES -- $ _____
DAYCARE / BABYSITTER --- $ _____
School SUPPLIES --------- $ _____
SCHOOL CLUB(S) DUES / FEES -- $ _____
NEW CLOTHING --------- $ _____
ALLOWANCES --------- $ _____
OTHER LIVING EEXPENSES --- $ _____

TOTAL LIVING EXPENSES: $ _____

MONTHLY EXPENSES

PET EXPENSES

PET INSURANCE------------------$_____
PET FOOD----------------------$_____
VETERINARY APPOINTMENT(S)--$_____
NEW TOYS / TREATS---------$_____
PET SITTER / DAYCARE-----$_____
OTHER PET EXPENSES------$_____

TOTAL PET EXPENSES: $_____

TRANSPORTATION

AUTOMOBILE INSURANCE-----$_____
AUTOMOBILE PAYMENTS---$_____
MONTHLY FUEL COSTS------$_____
REPAIRS / MAINTENANCE--$_____
FARES / TICKETS / ETC.----$_____
OTHER TRANSPORTATION EXPENSES--$_____

TOTAL TRANSPORTATION: $_____

GIFT EXPENSES

MONTHLY BIRTHDAYS---------$_____
MONTHLY HOLIDAYS------$_____
OTHER GIFT EXPENSES--------$_____

TOTAL GIFT EXPENSES: $_____

MONTHLY EXPENSES

HOUSING EXPENSES

RENTER'S / HOMEOWNER'S INSURANCE---$_____
CLEANING SUPPLIES-------$_____
GARDENING SUPPLIES-------$_____
FURNISHINGS-------------$_____
LAUNDRY / DRY CLEANING-$_____
HOME MAINTENANCE / REPAIRS--$_____
HOUSEHOLD NECESSITIES----$_____
OTHER HOUSING EXPENSES---$_____

TOTAL HOUSING EXPENSES: $_____

RECREATION

VACATION(S)-------------$_____
DINING OUT------------$_____
ENTERTAINMENT--------$_____
SOCIAL EVENTS--------$_____
OTHER RECREATION EXPENESES---$_____

TOTAL RECREATION EXPENSES: $_____

SAVINGS

EMERGENCY FUND-----------$_____
EDUCATION FUND------$_____
RETIREMENT FUND----------$_____

TOTAL SAVINGS: $_____

May _____

MONTHLY EXPENSES

DEBTS

CREDIT CARD #1 ---------- $ _____
CREDIT CARD #2 ---------- $ _____
CREDIT CARD #3 ---------- $ _____
CREDIT CARD #4 ---------- $ _____
PRIVATE DEBTS --------- $ _____
OTHER DEBTS ---------- $ _____

TOTAL DEBTS: $ _____

OTHER EXPENSES

OTHER EXPENSE #1 ---------- $ _____
OTHER EXPENSE #2 ---------- $ _____
OTHER EXPENSE #3 ---------- $ _____

TOTAL OTHER EXPENSES: $ _____

MONTHLY BUDGET

TOTAL INCOME: $ _____
— TOTAL EXPENSES: $ _____
_____
MONEY REMAINING: $ _____

MONTHLY NOTES

_____
_____
_____
_____
_____
_____
_____
_____
_____
_____
_____
_____
_____
_____
_____
_____
_____
_____
_____
_____
_____
_____
_____
_____
_____
_____

May

MONTHLY BILL TRACKING

PAID	BILL NAME	DUE DATE	AMOUNT DUE	AMOUNT PAID	BALANCE	PAYMENT METHOD / NOTES
○						
○						
○						
○						
○						
○						
○						
○						
○						
○						
○						
○						
○						
○						
○						
○						
○						
○						
○						
○						
○						
○						
○						
○						
○						
○						
○						
○						

Create Your June Budget Here

MONTHLY INCOMES

#	SOURCE	AMOUNT	DATE
1.		$	
2.		$	
3.		$	
4.		$	
5.		$	

TOTAL INCOME: $_____

> *Money is a terrible master but an excellent servant.*
> *-P.T. Barnum*

MONTHLY EXPENSES
UTILITIES

RENT / MORTGAGE----------$____
ELECTRICITY BILL----------$____
WATER BILL--------------$____
SEWAGE / TRASH----------$____
CABLE BILL--------------$____
INTERNET--------------$____
Phone Bill(s)------------$____

TOTAL UTILITIES: $_____

MONTHLY EXPENSES
HEALTHCARE

HEALTH INSURANCE----------$____
LIFE INSURANCE----------$____
DENTAL INSURANCE--------$____
DOCTOR APPOINTMENT(S)-$____
DENTAL APPOINTMENT(S)-$____
OPTOMETRY APPOINTMENT(S)-$____
PERSCRIPTIONS----------$____
OTHER MEDICAL EXPENSES---$____

TOTAL HEALTHCARE: $_____

LIVING EXPENSES

GROCERIES-------------$____
BEAUTY SUPPLIES---------$____
BEAUTY APPOINTMENTS----$____
MEMBERSHIP DUES / FEES--$____
DAYCARE / BABYSITTER----$____
School SUPPLIES---------$____
SCHOOL CLUB(S) DUES / FEES--$____
NEW CLOTHING----------$____
ALLOWANCES-----------$____
OTHER LIVING EXPENSES----$____

TOTAL LIVING EXPENSES: $_____

MONTHLY EXPENSES

PET EXPENSES

PET INSURANCE---------------- $_____
PET FOOD-------------------- $_____
VETERINARY APPOINTMENT(S)--$_____
NEW TOYS / TREATS----------- $_____
PET SITTER / DAYCARE------$_____
OTHER PET EXPENSES------ $_____

TOTAL PET EXPENSES: $_____

TRANSPORTATION

AUTOMOBILE INSURANCE----$_____
AUTOMOBILE PAYMENTS---$_____
MONTHLY FUEL COSTS------$_____
REPAIRS / MAINTENANCE--$_____
FARES / TICKETS /ETC.----$_____
OTHER TRANSPORTATION EXPENSES--$_____

TOTAL TRANSPORTATION: $_____

GIFT EXPENSES

MONTHLY BIRTHDAYS----------- $_____
MONTHLY HOLIDAYS------- $_____
OTHER GIFT EXPENSES--- $_____

TOTAL GIFT EXPENSES: $_____

MONTHLY EXPENSES

HOUSING EXPENSES

RENTER'S / HOMEOWNER'S INSURANCE---$_____
CLEANING SUPPLIES------ $_____
GARDENING SUPPLIES------ $_____
FURNISHINGS----------- $_____
LAUNDRY / DRY CLEANING-$_____
HOME MAINTENANCE / REPAIRS--$_____
HOUSEHOLD NECESSITIES----$_____
OTHER HOUSING EXPENSES---$_____

TOTAL HOUSING EXPENSES: $_____

RECREATION

VACATION(S)------------- $_____
DINING OUT----------- $_____
ENTERTAINMENT------- $_____
SOCIAL EVENTS--------- $_____
OTHER RECREATION EXPENESES---$_____

TOTAL RECREATION EXPENSES: $_____

SAVINGS

EMERGENCY FUND----------- $_____
EDUCATION FUND------- $_____
RETIREMENT FUND------- $_____

TOTAL SAVINGS: $_____

June _____

MONTHLY EXPENSES

DEBTS

CREDIT CARD #1 ----------- $ _____
CREDIT CARD #2 ----------- $ _____
CREDIT CARD #3 ----------- $ _____
CREDIT CARD #4 ----------- $ _____
PRIVATE DEBTS ----------- $ _____
OTHER DEBTS ----------- $ _____

TOTAL DEBTS: $ _____

OTHER EXPENSES

OTHER EXPENSE #1 -------- $ _____
OTHER EXPENSE #2 -------- $ _____
OTHER EXPENSE #3 -------- $ _____

TOTAL OTHER EXPENSES: $ _____

MONTHLY BUDGET

TOTAL INCOME: $ _____
– TOTAL EXPENSES: $ _____

MONEY REMAINING: $ _____

MONTHLY NOTES

_____
_____
_____
_____
_____
_____
_____
_____
_____
_____
_____
_____
_____
_____
_____
_____
_____
_____
_____
_____
_____
_____
_____
_____
_____
_____

June_____

MONTHLY BILL TRACKING

PAID	BILL NAME	DUE DATE	AMOUNT DUE	AMOUNT PAID	BALANCE	PAYMENT METHOD / NOTES
⭘						
⭘						
⭘						
⭘						
⭘						
⭘						
⭘						
⭘						
⭘						
⭘						
⭘						
⭘						
⭘						
⭘						
⭘						
⭘						
⭘						
⭘						
⭘						
⭘						
⭘						
⭘						
⭘						
⭘						
⭘						
⭘						
⭘						

Create Your July Budget Here

MONTHLY INCOMES

#	SOURCE	AMOUNT	DATE
1.		$	
2.		$	
3.		$	
4.		$	
5.		$	

TOTAL INCOME: $ _____

A journey of a thousand miles must begin with a single step.
-Lao Tzu

MONTHLY EXPENSES
UTILITIES

RENT / MORTGAGE --------- $ _____
ELECTRICITY BILL --------- $ _____
WATER BILL --------- $ _____
SEWAGE / TRASH --------- $ _____
CABLE BILL --------- $ _____
INTERNET --------- $ _____
PHONE BILL(S) --------- $ _____

TOTAL UTILITIES: $ _____

MONTHLY EXPENSES
HEALTHCARE

HEALTH INSURANCE --------- $ _____
LIFE INSURANCE --------- $ _____
DENTAL INSURANCE --------- $ _____
DOCTOR APPOINTMENT(S) - $ _____
DENTAL APPOINTMENT(S) - $ _____
OPTOMETRY APPOINTMENT(S) - $ _____
PERSCRIPTIONS --------- $ _____
OTHER MEDICAL EXPENSES --- $ _____

TOTAL HEALTHCARE: $ _____

LIVING EXPENSES

GROCERIES --------- $ _____
BEAUTY SUPPLIES --------- $ _____
BEAUTY APPOINTMENTS --- $ _____
MEMBERSHIP DUES / FEES -- $ _____
DAYCARE / BABYSITTER --- $ _____
SCHOOL SUPPLIES --------- $ _____
SCHOOL CLUB(S) DUES / FEES -- $ _____
NEW CLOTHING --------- $ _____
ALLOWANCES --------- $ _____
OTHER LIVING EXPENSES --- $ _____

TOTAL LIVING EXPENSES: $ _____

MONTHLY EXPENSES

PET EXPENSES

PET INSURANCE---------------- $ ____
PET FOOD---------------------- $ ____
VETERINARY APPOINTMENT(S)-- $ ____
NEW TOYS / TREATS ---------- $ ____
PET SITTER / DAYCARE----- $ ____
OTHER PET EXPENSES------ $ ____

TOTAL PET EXPENSES: $ ____

TRANSPORTATION

AUTOMOBILE INSURANCE---- $ ____
AUTOMOBILE PAYMENTS--- $ ____
MONTHLY FUEL COSTS----- $ ____
REPAIRS / MAINTENANCE-- $ ____
FARES / TICKETS / ETC.---- $ ____
OTHER TRANSPORTATION EXPENSES-- $ ____

TOTAL TRANSPORTATION: $ ____

GIFT EXPENSES

MONTHLY BIRTHDAYS--------- $ ____
MONTHLY HOLIDAYS------ $ ____
OTHER GIFT EXPENSES--- $ ____

TOTAL GIFT EXPENSES: $ ____

MONTHLY EXPENSES

HOUSING EXPENSES

RENTER'S / HOMEOWNER'S INSURANCE--- $ ____
CLEANING SUPPLIES------ $ ____
GARDENING SUPPLIES------ $ ____
FURNISHINGS------------- $ ____
LAUNDRY / DRY CLEANING- $ ____
HOME MAINTENANCE / REPAIRS-- $ ____
HOUSEHOLD NECESSITIES---- $ ____
OTHER HOUSING EXPENSES--- $ ____

TOTAL HOUSING EXPENSES: $ ____

RECREATION

VACATION(S)------------- $ ____
DINING OUT------------- $ ____
ENTERTAINMENT--------- $ ____
SOCIAL EVENTS--------- $ ____
OTHER RECREATION EXPENSES--- $ ____

TOTAL RECREATION EXPENSES: $ ____

SAVINGS

EMERGENCY FUND----------- $ ____
EDUCATION FUND------- $ ____
RETIREMENT FUND------- $ ____

TOTAL SAVINGS: $ ____

July _____

MONTHLY EXPENSES

DEBTS

CREDIT CARD #1 --------- $ _____
CREDIT CARD #2 --------- $ _____
CREDIT CARD # 3 --------- $ _____
CREDIT CARD # 4 --------- $ _____
PRIVATE DEBTS -------- $ _____
OTHER DEBTS --------- $ _____

TOTAL DEBTS : $ _____

OTHER EXPENSES

OTHER EXPENSE #1 -------- $ _____
OTHER EXPENSE #2 -------- $ _____
OTHER EXPENSE #3 -------- $ _____

TOTAL OTHER EXPENSES : $ _____

MONTHLY BUDGET

TOTAL INCOME : $ _____
— TOTAL EXPENSES : $ _____
_____
MONEY REMAINING : $ _____

MONTHLY NOTES

_____
_____
_____
_____
_____
_____
_____
_____
_____
_____
_____
_____
_____
_____
_____
_____
_____
_____
_____
_____
_____
_____
_____
_____
_____
_____
_____
_____
_____

July _____

MONTHLY BILL TRACKING

PAID	BILL NAME	DUE DATE	AMOUNT DUE	AMOUNT PAID	BALANCE	PAYMENT METHOD / NOTES
○						
○						
○						
○						
○						
○						
○						
○						
○						
○						
○						
○						
○						
○						
○						
○						
○						
○						
○						
○						
○						
○						
○						
○						
○						
○						
○						

Create Your August Budget Here

MONTHLY INCOMES

#	SOURCE	AMOUNT	DATE
1.		$	
2.		$	
3.		$	
4.		$	
5.		$	

TOTAL INCOME: $_____

Fortune sides with him who dares.
-Virgil

MONTHLY EXPENSES
UTILITIES

RENT / MORTGAGE----------$____
ELECTRICITY BILL--------$____
WATER BILL----------$____
SEWAGE / TRASH--------$____
CABLE BILL----------$____
INTERNET--------$____
PHONE BILL(S)--------$____

TOTAL UTILITIES: $_____

MONTHLY EXPENSES
HEALTHCARE

HEALTH INSURANCE----------$____
LIFE INSURANCE----------$____
DENTAL INSURANCE--------$____
DOCTOR APPOINTMENT(S)-$____
DENTAL APPOINTMENT(S)-$____
OPTOMETRY APPOINTMENT(S)-$____
PERSCRIPTIONS----------$____
OTHER MEDICAL EXPENSES---$____

TOTAL HEALTHCARE: $_____

LIVING EXPENSES

GROCERIES----------$____
BEAUTY SUPPLIES--------$____
BEAUTY APPOINTMENTS----$____
MEMBERSHIP DUES / FEES--$____
DAYCARE / BABYSITTER----$____
SCHOOL SUPPLIES--------$____
SCHOOL CLUB(S) DUES / FEES--$____
NEW CLOTHING----------$____
ALLOWANCES----------$____
OTHER LIVING EXPENSES----$____

TOTAL LIVING EXPENSES: $_____

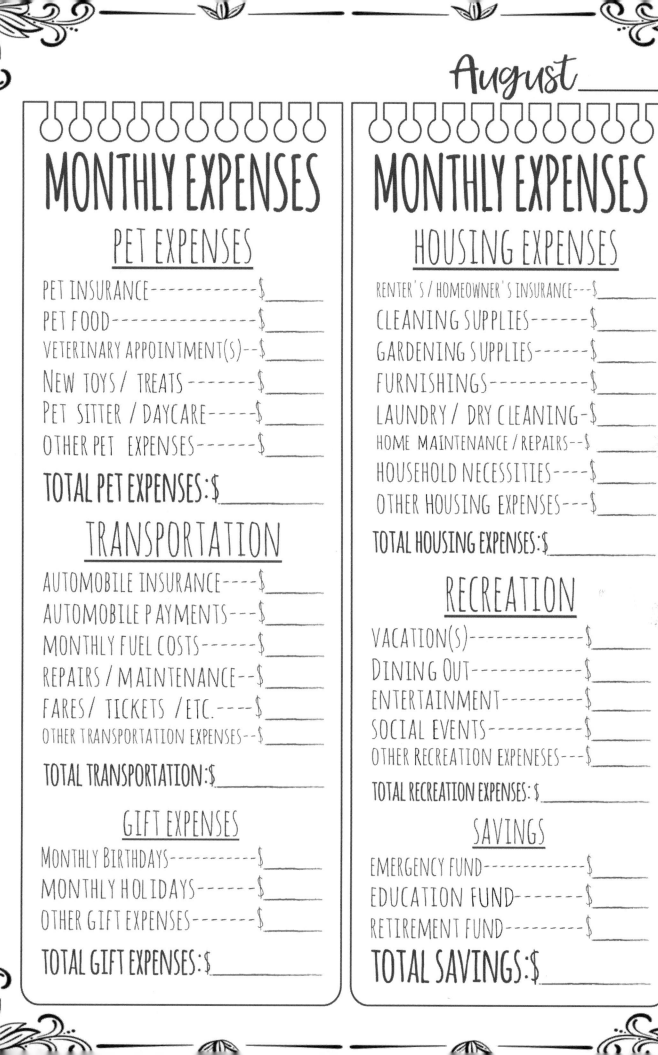

MONTHLY EXPENSES

PET EXPENSES

PET INSURANCE ---------- $ ____
PET FOOD -------------- $ ____
VETERINARY APPOINTMENT(S) -- $ ____
NEW TOYS / TREATS ------- $ ____
PET SITTER / DAYCARE ----- $ ____
OTHER PET EXPENSES ----- $ ____

TOTAL PET EXPENSES: $ ____

TRANSPORTATION

AUTOMOBILE INSURANCE ---- $ ____
AUTOMOBILE PAYMENTS --- $ ____
MONTHLY FUEL COSTS ------ $ ____
REPAIRS / MAINTENANCE -- $ ____
FARES / TICKETS / ETC. ----- $ ____
OTHER TRANSPORTATION EXPENSES -- $ ____

TOTAL TRANSPORTATION: $ ____

GIFT EXPENSES

MONTHLY BIRTHDAYS --------- $ ____
MONTHLY HOLIDAYS ------ $ ____
OTHER GIFT EXPENSES --- $ ____

TOTAL GIFT EXPENSES: $ ____

MONTHLY EXPENSES

HOUSING EXPENSES

RENTER'S / HOMEOWNER'S INSURANCE --- $ ____
CLEANING SUPPLIES ------ $ ____
GARDENING SUPPLIES ------ $ ____
FURNISHINGS ----------- $ ____
LAUNDRY / DRY CLEANING - $ ____
HOME MAINTENANCE / REPAIRS -- $ ____
HOUSEHOLD NECESSITIES ---- $ ____
OTHER HOUSING EXPENSES --- $ ____

TOTAL HOUSING EXPENSES: $ ____

RECREATION

VACATION(S) ----------- $ ____
DINING OUT ----------- $ ____
ENTERTAINMENT --------- $ ____
SOCIAL EVENTS --------- $ ____
OTHER RECREATION EXPENESES --- $ ____

TOTAL RECREATION EXPENSES: $ ____

SAVINGS

EMERGENCY FUND ---------- $ ____
EDUCATION FUND ------- $ ____
RETIREMENT FUND ------- $ ____

TOTAL SAVINGS: $ ____

MONTHLY EXPENSES

DEBTS

CREDIT CARD #1 ------------- $ _____
CREDIT CARD #2 ------------- $ _____
CREDIT CARD # 3 ------------ $ _____
CREDIT CARD #4 ----------- $ _____
PRIVATE DEBTS ----------- $ _____
OTHER DEBTS ----------- $ _____

TOTAL DEBTS: $ _____

OTHER EXPENSES

OTHER EXPENSE #1 ----------- $ _____
OTHER EXPENSE #2 ----------- $ _____
OTHER EXPENSE #3 ----------- $ _____

TOTAL OTHER EXPENSES: $ _____

MONTHLY BUDGET

TOTAL INCOME: $ _____
— TOTAL EXPENSES: $ _____
_____
MONEY REMAINING: $ _____

MONTHLY NOTES

_____
_____
_____
_____
_____
_____
_____
_____
_____
_____
_____
_____
_____
_____
_____
_____
_____
_____
_____
_____
_____
_____
_____
_____
_____

MONTHLY BILL TRACKING

August _____

PAID	BILL NAME	DUE DATE	AMOUNT DUE	AMOUNT PAID	BALANCE	PAYMENT METHOD / NOTES
○						
○						
○						
○						
○						
○						
○						
○						
○						
○						
○						
○						
○						
○						
○						
○						
○						
○						
○						
○						
○						
○						
○						
○						
○						
○						

Create Your September Budget Here

MONTHLY INCOMES

#	SOURCE	AMOUNT	DATE
1.		$	
2.		$	
3.		$	
4.		$	
5.		$	

TOTAL INCOME: $_____

> *No wealth can ever make a bad man at peace with himself.*
> *–Plato*

MONTHLY EXPENSES
UTILITIES

RENT / MORTGAGE---------- $ _____
ELECTRICITY BILL---------- $ _____
WATER BILL---------- $ _____
SEWAGE / TRASH---------- $ _____
CABLE BILL---------- $ _____
INTERNET---------- $ _____
PHONE BILL(S)---------- $ _____

TOTAL UTILITIES: $_____

MONTHLY EXPENSES
HEALTHCARE

HEALTH INSURANCE---------- $ _____
LIFE INSURANCE---------- $ _____
DENTAL INSURANCE-------- $ _____
DOCTOR APPOINTMENT(S)- $ _____
DENTAL APPOINTMENT(S)- $ _____
OPTOMETRY APPOINTMENT(S)- $ _____
PERSCRIPTIONS---------- $ _____
OTHER MEDICAL EXPENSES--- $ _____

TOTAL HEALTHCARE: $_____

LIVING EXPENSES

GROCERIES---------- $ _____
BEAUTY SUPPLIES---------- $ _____
BEAUTY APPOINTMENTS---- $ _____
MEMBERSHIP DUES / FEES-- $ _____
DAYCARE / BABYSITTER ---- $ _____
SCHOOL SUPPLIES---------- $ _____
SCHOOL CLUB(S) DUES / FEES-- $ _____
NEW CLOTHING---------- $ _____
ALLOWANCES---------- $ _____
OTHER LIVING EXPENSES---- $ _____

TOTAL LIVING EXPENSES: $_____

MONTHLY EXPENSES

PET EXPENSES

PET INSURANCE --------------- $ ____
PET FOOD ------------------ $ ____
VETERINARY APPOINTMENT(S) -- $ ____
New TOYS / TREATS --------- $ ____
Pet SITTER / DAYCARE ------ $ ____
OTHER PET EXPENSES ------- $ ____

TOTAL PET EXPENSES: $ ____

TRANSPORTATION

AUTOMOBILE INSURANCE ----- $ ____
AUTOMOBILE PAYMENTS --- $ ____
MONTHLY FUEL COSTS ------ $ ____
REPAIRS / MAINTENANCE -- $ ____
FARES / TICKETS / ETC. ----- $ ____
OTHER TRANSPORTATION EXPENSES -- $ ____

TOTAL TRANSPORTATION: $ ____

GIFT EXPENSES

Monthly Birthdays --------- $ ____
MONTHLY HOLIDAYS ------ $ ____
OTHER GIFT EXPENSES ------- $ ____

TOTAL GIFT EXPENSES: $ ____

MONTHLY EXPENSES

HOUSING EXPENSES

RENTER'S / HOMEOWNER'S INSURANCE --- $ ____
CLEANING SUPPLIES ------ $ ____
GARDENING SUPPLIES -------- $ ____
FURNISHINGS ----------- $ ____
LAUNDRY / DRY CLEANING - $ ____
HOME MAINTENANCE / REPAIRS -- $ ____
HOUSEHOLD NECESSITIES ---- $ ____
OTHER HOUSING EXPENSES --- $ ____

TOTAL HOUSING EXPENSES: $ ____

RECREATION

VACATION(S) ------------- $ ____
DINING OUT ----------- $ ____
ENTERTAINMENT --------- $ ____
SOCIAL EVENTS --------- $ ____
OTHER RECREATION EXPENESES --- $ ____

TOTAL RECREATION EXPENSES: $ ____

SAVINGS

EMERGENCY FUND ----------- $ ____
EDUCATION FUND ------- $ ____
RETIREMENT FUND -------- $ ____

TOTAL SAVINGS: $ ____

September_____

MONTHLY EXPENSES

DEBTS

CREDIT CARD #1 ----------- $____
CREDIT CARD #2 ----------- $____
CREDIT CARD #3 ----------- $____
CREDIT CARD #4 ----------- $____
PRIVATE DEBTS ----------- $____
OTHER DEBTS ----------- $____

TOTAL DEBTS: $____

OTHER EXPENSES

OTHER EXPENSE #1 -------- $____
OTHER EXPENSE #2 -------- $____
OTHER EXPENSE #3 -------- $____

TOTAL OTHER EXPENSES: $____

MONTHLY BUDGET

TOTAL INCOME: $____
− TOTAL EXPENSES: $____

MONEY REMAINING: $____

MONTHLY NOTES

September

MONTHLY BILL TRACKING

PAID	BILL NAME	DUE DATE	AMOUNT DUE	AMOUNT PAID	BALANCE	PAYMENT METHOD / NOTES
○						
○						
○						
○						
○						
○						
○						
○						
○						
○						
○						
○						
○						
○						
○						
○						
○						
○						
○						
○						
○						
○						
○						
○						
○						
○						
○						

Create Your October Budget Here

MONTHLY INCOMES

#	SOURCE	AMOUNT	DATE
1.		$	
2.		$	
3.		$	
4.		$	
5.		$	

TOTAL INCOME: $ _____

> *Do not go where the path may lead, go instead where there is no path and leave a trail.*
> *—Ralph Waldo Emerson*

MONTHLY EXPENSES
UTILITIES

RENT / MORTGAGE ---------- $ _____
ELECTRICITY BILL ---------- $ _____
WATER BILL ---------- $ _____
SEWAGE / TRASH ---------- $ _____
CABLE BILL ---------- $ _____
INTERNET ---------- $ _____
PHONE BILL(S) ---------- $ _____

TOTAL UTILITIES: $ _____

MONTHLY EXPENSES
HEALTHCARE

HEALTH INSURANCE ---------- $ _____
LIFE INSURANCE ---------- $ _____
DENTAL INSURANCE -------- $ _____
DOCTOR APPOINTMENT(S) - $ _____
DENTAL APPOINTMENT(S) - $ _____
OPTOMETRY APPOINTMENT(S) - $ _____
PERSCRIPTIONS ---------- $ _____
OTHER MEDICAL EXPENSES --- $ _____

TOTAL HEALTHCARE: $ _____

LIVING EXPENSES

GROCERIES ---------- $ _____
BEAUTY SUPPLIES ---------- $ _____
BEAUTY APPOINTMENTS ---- $ _____
MEMBERSHIP DUES / FEES -- $ _____
DAYCARE / BABYSITTER ---- $ _____
SCHOOL SUPPLIES ---------- $ _____
SCHOOL CLUB(S) DUES / FEES -- $ _____
NEW CLOTHING ---------- $ _____
ALLOWANCES ---------- $ _____
OTHER LIVING EXPENSES ---- $ _____

TOTAL LIVING EXPENSES: $ _____

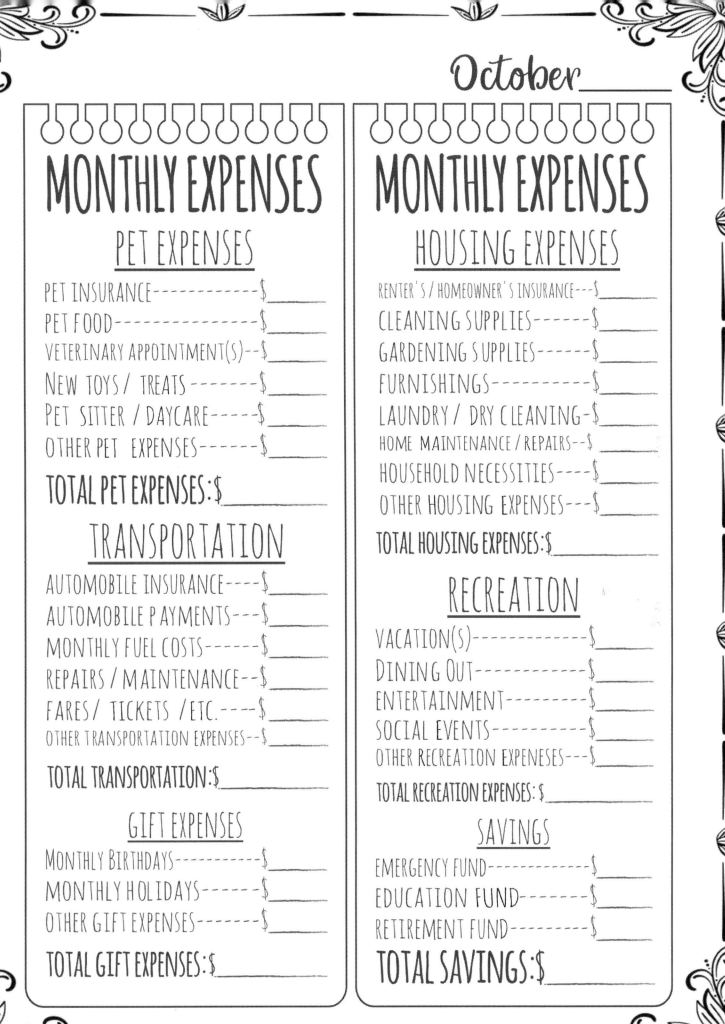

October _____

MONTHLY EXPENSES
PET EXPENSES

PET INSURANCE------------- $ _____
PET FOOD------------------- $ _____
VETERINARY APPOINTMENT(S)-- $ _____
NEW TOYS / TREATS --------- $ _____
PET SITTER / DAYCARE------ $ _____
OTHER PET EXPENSES------- $ _____

TOTAL PET EXPENSES: $ _____

TRANSPORTATION

AUTOMOBILE INSURANCE----- $ _____
AUTOMOBILE PAYMENTS--- $ _____
MONTHLY FUEL COSTS------ $ _____
REPAIRS / MAINTENANCE-- $ _____
FARES / TICKETS / ETC.----- $ _____
OTHER TRANSPORTATION EXPENSES-- $ _____

TOTAL TRANSPORTATION: $ _____

GIFT EXPENSES

MONTHLY BIRTHDAYS----------- $ _____
MONTHLY HOLIDAYS------ $ _____
OTHER GIFT EXPENSES------- $ _____

TOTAL GIFT EXPENSES: $ _____

MONTHLY EXPENSES
HOUSING EXPENSES

RENTER'S / HOMEOWNER'S INSURANCE---$ _____
CLEANING SUPPLIES------- $ _____
GARDENING SUPPLIES------- $ _____
FURNISHINGS----------- $ _____
LAUNDRY / DRY CLEANING-$ _____
HOME MAINTENANCE / REPAIRS--$ _____
HOUSEHOLD NECESSITIES----$ _____
OTHER HOUSING EXPENSES---$ _____

TOTAL HOUSING EXPENSES: $ _____

RECREATION

VACATION(S)------------- $ _____
DINING OUT----------- $ _____
ENTERTAINMENT-------- $ _____
SOCIAL EVENTS-------- $ _____
OTHER RECREATION EXPENESES---$ _____

TOTAL RECREATION EXPENSES: $ _____

SAVINGS

EMERGENCY FUND------------ $ _____
EDUCATION FUND------ $ _____
RETIREMENT FUND-------- $ _____

TOTAL SAVINGS: $ _____

MONTHLY EXPENSES

DEBTS

CREDIT CARD #1 ------------ $_____
CREDIT CARD #2 ------------ $_____
CREDIT CARD # 3 ----------- $_____
CREDIT CARD #4 ------------ $_____
PRIVATE DEBTS ------------ $_____
OTHER DEBTS ------------- $_____

TOTAL DEBTS: $_____

OTHER EXPENSES

OTHER EXPENSE #1 --------- $_____
OTHER EXPENSE #2 --------- $_____
OTHER EXPENSE #3 --------- $_____

TOTAL OTHER EXPENSES: $_____

MONTHLY BUDGET

TOTAL INCOME: $_____
— TOTAL EXPENSES: $_____
_____
MONEY REMAINING: $_____

MONTHLY NOTES

October

MONTHLY BILL TRACKING

PAID	BILL NAME	DUE DATE	AMOUNT DUE	AMOUNT PAID	BALANCE	PAYMENT METHOD / NOTES
○						
○						
○						
○						
○						
○						
○						
○						
○						
○						
○						
○						
○						
○						
○						
○						
○						
○						
○						
○						
○						
○						
○						
○						
○						
○						
○						
○						

Create Your November Budget Here

MONTHLY INCOMES

#	SOURCE	AMOUNT	DATE
1.		$	
2.		$	
3.		$	
4.		$	
5.		$	

TOTAL INCOME: $ _____

Let no feeling of discouragement prey upon you, and in the end you are sure to succeed.
—Abraham Lincoln

MONTHLY EXPENSES
UTILITIES

RENT / MORTGAGE ---------- $ _____
ELECTRICITY BILL ---------- $ _____
WATER BILL ---------- $ _____
SEWAGE / TRASH ---------- $ _____
CABLE BILL ---------- $ _____
INTERNET ---------- $ _____
PHONE BILL(S) ---------- $ _____

TOTAL UTILITIES: $ _____

MONTHLY EXPENSES
HEALTHCARE

HEALTH INSURANCE ---------- $ _____
LIFE INSURANCE ---------- $ _____
DENTAL INSURANCE -------- $ _____
DOCTOR APPOINTMENT(S) - $ _____
DENTAL APPOINTMENT(S) - $ _____
OPTOMETRY APPOINTMENT(S) - $ _____
PERSCRIPTIONS ---------- $ _____
OTHER MEDICAL EXPENSES --- $ _____

TOTAL HEALTHCARE: $ _____

LIVING EXPENSES

GROCERIES ---------- $ _____
BEAUTY SUPPLIES ---------- $ _____
BEAUTY APPOINTMENTS ---- $ _____
MEMBERSHIP DUES / FEES -- $ _____
DAYCARE / BABYSITTER ---- $ _____
SCHOOL SUPPLIES ---------- $ _____
SCHOOL CLUB(S) DUES / FEES -- $ _____
NEW CLOTHING ---------- $ _____
ALLOWANCES ---------- $ _____
OTHER LIVING EXPENSES ---- $ _____

TOTAL LIVING EXPENSES: $ _____

MONTHLY EXPENSES

PET EXPENSES

PET INSURANCE------------- $_____
PET FOOD--------------------- $_____
VETERINARY APPOINTMENT(S)-- $_____
NEW TOYS / TREATS --------- $_____
PET SITTER / DAYCARE----- $_____
OTHER PET EXPENSES------ $_____

TOTAL PET EXPENSES: $_____

TRANSPORTATION

AUTOMOBILE INSURANCE---- $_____
AUTOMOBILE PAYMENTS--- $_____
MONTHLY FUEL COSTS------ $_____
REPAIRS / MAINTENANCE-- $_____
FARES / TICKETS / ETC.---- $_____
OTHER TRANSPORTATION EXPENSES--$_____

TOTAL TRANSPORTATION: $_____

GIFT EXPENSES

MONTHLY BIRTHDAYS--------- $_____
MONTHLY HOLIDAYS------ $_____
OTHER GIFT EXPENSES------- $_____

TOTAL GIFT EXPENSES: $_____

MONTHLY EXPENSES

HOUSING EXPENSES

RENTER'S / HOMEOWNER'S INSURANCE--- $_____
CLEANING SUPPLIES------- $_____
GARDENING SUPPLIES------ $_____
FURNISHINGS------------- $_____
LAUNDRY / DRY CLEANING- $_____
HOME MAINTENANCE / REPAIRS-- $_____
HOUSEHOLD NECESSITIES---- $_____
OTHER HOUSING EXPENSES--- $_____

TOTAL HOUSING EXPENSES: $_____

RECREATION

VACATION(S)------------- $_____
DINING OUT------------- $_____
ENTERTAINMENT--------- $_____
SOCIAL EVENTS--------- $_____
OTHER RECREATION EXPENESES--- $_____

TOTAL RECREATION EXPENSES: $_____

SAVINGS

EMERGENCY FUND----------- $_____
EDUCATION FUND------ $_____
RETIREMENT FUND--------- $_____

TOTAL SAVINGS: $_____

MONTHLY EXPENSES

DEBTS

CREDIT CARD #1 ----------- $ _____
CREDIT CARD #2 ----------- $ _____
CREDIT CARD # 3 ----------- $ _____
CREDIT CARD #4 ----------- $ _____
PRIVATE DEBTS ----------- $ _____
OTHER DEBTS ----------- $ _____

TOTAL DEBTS: $ _____

OTHER EXPENSES

OTHER EXPENSE #1 --------- $ _____
OTHER EXPENSE #2 --------- $ _____
OTHER EXPENSE #3 --------- $ _____

TOTAL OTHER EXPENSES: $ _____

MONTHLY BUDGET

TOTAL INCOME: $ _____
− TOTAL EXPENSES: $ _____

MONEY REMAINING: $ _____

MONTHLY NOTES

_____
_____
_____
_____
_____
_____
_____
_____
_____
_____
_____
_____
_____
_____
_____
_____
_____
_____
_____
_____
_____
_____
_____
_____
_____
_____
_____
_____

November

MONTHLY BILL TRACKING

PAID	BILL NAME	DUE DATE	AMOUNT DUE	AMOUNT PAID	BALANCE	PAYMENT METHOD / NOTES
○						
○						
○						
○						
○						
○						
○						
○						
○						
○						
○						
○						
○						
○						
○						
○						
○						
○						
○						
○						
○						
○						
○						
○						
○						

Create Your December Budget Here

MONTHLY INCOMES

#	SOURCE	AMOUNT	DATE
1.		$	
2.		$	
3.		$	
4.		$	
5.		$	

TOTAL INCOME: $_____

> Live as if you were to die tomorrow.
> Learn as if you were to live forever.
> -Mahatma Gandhi

MONTHLY EXPENSES
UTILITIES

RENT / MORTGAGE---------$_____
ELECTRICITY BILL----------$_____
WATER BILL--------------$_____
SEWAGE / TRASH----------$_____
CABLE BILL-------------$_____
INTERNET--------------$_____
PHONE BILL(S)----------$_____

TOTAL UTILITIES: $_____

MONTHLY EXPENSES
HEALTHCARE

HEALTH INSURANCE----------$_____
LIFE INSURANCE-----------$_____
DENTAL INSURANCE---------$_____
DOCTOR APPOINTMENT(S)-$_____
DENTAL APPOINTMENT(S)-$_____
OPTOMETRY APPOINTMENT(S)-$_____
PERSCRIPTIONS------------$_____
OTHER MEDICAL EXPENSES---$_____

TOTAL HEALTHCARE: $_____

LIVING EXPENSES

GROCERIES---------------$_____
BEAUTY SUPPLIES----------$_____
BEAUTY APPOINTMENTS----$_____
MEMBERSHIP DUES / FEES--$_____
DAYCARE / BABYSITTER ----$_____
SCHOOL SUPPLIES----------$_____
SCHOOL CLUB(S) DUES / FEES--$_____
NEW CLOTHING-----------$_____
ALLOWANCES------------$_____
OTHER LIVING EXPENSES----$_____

TOTAL LIVING EXPENSES: $_____

MONTHLY EXPENSES

PET EXPENSES

PET INSURANCE----------$_____

PET FOOD----------$_____

VETERINARY APPOINTMENT(S)--$_____

NEW TOYS / TREATS-------$_____

PET SITTER / DAYCARE-----$_____

OTHER PET EXPENSES------$_____

TOTAL PET EXPENSES:$_____

TRANSPORTATION

AUTOMOBILE INSURANCE----$_____

AUTOMOBILE PAYMENTS---$_____

MONTHLY FUEL COSTS------$_____

REPAIRS / MAINTENANCE--$_____

FARES / TICKETS / ETC.----$_____

OTHER TRANSPORTATION EXPENSES--$_____

TOTAL TRANSPORTATION:$_____

GIFT EXPENSES

MONTHLY BIRTHDAYS----------$_____

MONTHLY HOLIDAYS--------$_____

OTHER GIFT EXPENSES-------$_____

TOTAL GIFT EXPENSES:$_____

MONTHLY EXPENSES

HOUSING EXPENSES

RENTER'S / HOMEOWNER'S INSURANCE---$_____

CLEANING SUPPLIES------$_____

GARDENING SUPPLIES------$_____

FURNISHINGS----------$_____

LAUNDRY / DRY CLEANING-$_____

HOME MAINTENANCE / REPAIRS--$_____

HOUSEHOLD NECESSITIES----$_____

OTHER HOUSING EXPENSES---$_____

TOTAL HOUSING EXPENSES:$_____

RECREATION

VACATION(S)----------$_____

DINING OUT----------$_____

ENTERTAINMENT--------$_____

SOCIAL EVENTS--------$_____

OTHER RECREATION EXPENESES---$_____

TOTAL RECREATION EXPENSES: $_____

SAVINGS

EMERGENCY FUND----------$_____

EDUCATION FUND-------$_____

RETIREMENT FUND--------$_____

TOTAL SAVINGS:$_____

December_____

MONTHLY EXPENSES

DEBTS

CREDIT CARD #1 --------- $ ____
CREDIT CARD #2 --------- $ ____
CREDIT CARD # 3 --------- $ ____
CREDIT CARD #4 --------- $ ____
PRIVATE DEBTS --------- $ ____
OTHER DEBTS --------- $ ____

TOTAL DEBTS: $ _____

OTHER EXPENSES

OTHER EXPENSE #1 --------- $ ____
OTHER EXPENSE #2 --------- $ ____
OTHER EXPENSE #3 --------- $ ____

TOTAL OTHER EXPENSES: $ _____

MONTHLY BUDGET

TOTAL INCOME: $ _____
– TOTAL EXPENSES: $ _____
_____
MONEY REMAINING: $ _____

MONTHLY NOTES

_____
_____
_____
_____
_____
_____
_____
_____
_____
_____
_____
_____
_____
_____
_____
_____
_____
_____
_____
_____
_____
_____
_____
_____
_____
_____
_____
_____
_____
_____

December

MONTHLY BILL TRACKING

PAID	BILL NAME	DUE DATE	AMOUNT DUE	AMOUNT PAID	BALANCE	PAYMENT METHOD / NOTES
○						
○						
○						
○						
○						
○						
○						
○						
○						
○						
○						
○						
○						
○						
○						
○						
○						
○						
○						
○						
○						
○						
○						
○						
○						

Create Your January Budget Here

MONTHLY INCOMES

#	SOURCE	AMOUNT	DATE
1.		$	
2.		$	
3.		$	
4.		$	
5.		$	

TOTAL INCOME: $ _____

> Wealth consists not in having great possessions,
> but in having few wants.
> -Epictetus

MONTHLY EXPENSES
UTILITIES

RENT / MORTGAGE---------$ _____
ELECTRICITY BILL---------$ _____
WATER BILL-------------$ _____
SEWAGE / TRASH---------$ _____
CABLE BILL-------------$ _____
INTERNET-------------$ _____
PHONE BILL(S)----------$ _____

TOTAL UTILITIES: $ _____

MONTHLY EXPENSES
HEALTHCARE

HEALTH INSURANCE----------$ _____
LIFE INSURANCE-----------$ _____
DENTAL INSURANCE--------$ _____
DOCTOR APPOINTMENT(S)-$ _____
DENTAL APPOINTMENT(S)-$ _____
OPTOMETRY APPOINTMENT(S)-$ _____
PERSCRIPTIONS----------$ _____
OTHER MEDICAL EXPENSES---$ _____

TOTAL HEALTHCARE: $ _____

LIVING EXPENSES

GROCERIES--------------$ _____
BEAUTY SUPPLIES---------$ _____
BEAUTY APPOINTMENTS----$ _____
MEMBERSHIP DUES / FEES--$ _____
DAYCARE / BABYSITTER ----$ _____
School SUPPLIES----------$ _____
SCHOOL CLUB(S) DUES / FEES--$ _____
NEW CLOTHING----------$ _____
ALLOWANCES-----------$ _____
OTHER LIVING EXPENSES----$ _____

TOTAL LIVING EXPENSES: $ _____

January

MONTHLY EXPENSES
PET EXPENSES

PET INSURANCE----------$_____
PET FOOD-------------$_____
VETERINARY APPOINTMENT(S)--$_____
NEW TOYS / TREATS------$_____
PET SITTER / DAYCARE----$_____
OTHER PET EXPENSES-----$_____

TOTAL PET EXPENSES: $_____

TRANSPORTATION

AUTOMOBILE INSURANCE---$_____
AUTOMOBILE PAYMENTS---$_____
MONTHLY FUEL COSTS------$_____
REPAIRS / MAINTENANCE--$_____
FARES / TICKETS /ETC.----$_____
OTHER TRANSPORTATION EXPENSES--$_____

TOTAL TRANSPORTATION: $_____

GIFT EXPENSES

MONTHLY BIRTHDAYS--------$_____
MONTHLY HOLIDAYS-----$_____
OTHER GIFT EXPENSES----$_____

TOTAL GIFT EXPENSES: $_____

MONTHLY EXPENSES
HOUSING EXPENSES

RENTER'S / HOMEOWNER'S INSURANCE---$_____
CLEANING SUPPLIES------$_____
GARDENING SUPPLIES-----$_____
FURNISHINGS----------$_____
LAUNDRY / DRY CLEANING-$_____
HOME MAINTENANCE / REPAIRS--$_____
HOUSEHOLD NECESSITIES----$_____
OTHER HOUSING EXPENSES---$_____

TOTAL HOUSING EXPENSES: $_____

RECREATION

VACATION(S)-----------$_____
DINING OUT-----------$_____
ENTERTAINMENT--------$_____
SOCIAL EVENTS---------$_____
OTHER RECREATION EXPENESES---$_____

TOTAL RECREATION EXPENSES: $_____

SAVINGS

EMERGENCY FUND-----------$_____
EDUCATION FUND-------$_____
RETIREMENT FUND--------$_____

TOTAL SAVINGS: $_____

January _____

MONTHLY EXPENSES

DEBTS

CREDIT CARD #1 ----------- $ ____
CREDIT CARD #2 ----------- $ ____
CREDIT CARD #3 ----------- $ ____
CREDIT CARD #4 ----------- $ ____
PRIVATE DEBTS ----------- $ ____
OTHER DEBTS ----------- $ ____

TOTAL DEBTS: $ _____

OTHER EXPENSES

OTHER EXPENSE #1 ----------- $ ____
OTHER EXPENSE #2 ----------- $ ____
OTHER EXPENSE #3 ----------- $ ____

TOTAL OTHER EXPENSES: $ _____

MONTHLY BUDGET

TOTAL INCOME: $ _____
− TOTAL EXPENSES: $ _____
_____

MONEY REMAINING: $ _____

MONTHLY NOTES

_____
_____
_____
_____
_____
_____
_____
_____
_____
_____
_____
_____
_____
_____
_____
_____
_____
_____
_____
_____
_____
_____
_____
_____
_____
_____
_____
_____
_____

January

MONTHLY BILL TRACKING

PAID	BILL NAME	DUE DATE	AMOUNT DUE	AMOUNT PAID	BALANCE	PAYMENT METHOD / NOTES
◯						
◯						
◯						
◯						
◯						
◯						
◯						
◯						
◯						
◯						
◯						
◯						
◯						
◯						
◯						
◯						
◯						
◯						
◯						
◯						
◯						
◯						
◯						
◯						
◯						
◯						

Create Your February Budget Here

MONTHLY INCOMES

#	SOURCE	AMOUNT	DATE
1.		$	
2.		$	
3.		$	
4.		$	
5.		$	

TOTAL INCOME: $_____

Money often costs too much.
-Ralph Waldo Emerson

MONTHLY EXPENSES
UTILITIES

RENT / MORTGAGE---------- $_____
ELECTRICITY BILL---------- $_____
WATER BILL------------ $_____
SEWAGE / TRASH--------- $_____
CABLE BILL------------ $_____
INTERNET------------- $_____
PHONE BILL(S)---------- $_____

TOTAL UTILITIES: $_____

MONTHLY EXPENSES
HEALTHCARE

HEALTH INSURANCE---------- $_____
LIFE INSURANCE---------- $_____
DENTAL INSURANCE-------- $_____
DOCTOR APPOINTMENT(S)- $_____
DENTAL APPOINTMENT(S)- $_____
OPTOMETRY APPOINTMENT(S)- $_____
PERSCRIPTIONS--------- $_____
OTHER MEDICAL EXPENSES--- $_____

TOTAL HEALTHCARE: $_____

LIVING EXPENSES

GROCERIES------------ $_____
BEAUTY SUPPLIES--------- $_____
BEAUTY APPOINTMENTS---- $_____
MEMBERSHIP DUES / FEES-- $_____
DAYCARE / BABYSITTER ---- $_____
SCHOOL SUPPLIES-------- $_____
SCHOOL CLUB(S) DUES / FEES-- $_____
NEW CLOTHING---------- $_____
ALLOWANCES----------- $_____
OTHER LIVING EXPENSES---- $_____

TOTAL LIVING EXPENSES: $_____

MONTHLY EXPENSES
PET EXPENSES

PET INSURANCE------------ $ _____
PET FOOD---------------- $ _____
VETERINARY APPOINTMENT(S)-- $ _____
NEW TOYS / TREATS ------- $ _____
PET SITTER / DAYCARE----- $ _____
OTHER PET EXPENSES----- $ _____

TOTAL PET EXPENSES: $ _____

TRANSPORTATION

AUTOMOBILE INSURANCE---- $ _____
AUTOMOBILE PAYMENTS--- $ _____
MONTHLY FUEL COSTS----- $ _____
REPAIRS / MAINTENANCE-- $ _____
FARES / TICKETS / ETC.----- $ _____
OTHER TRANSPORTATION EXPENSES-- $ _____

TOTAL TRANSPORTATION: $ _____

GIFT EXPENSES

MONTHLY BIRTHDAYS--------- $ _____
MONTHLY HOLIDAYS------ $ _____
OTHER GIFT EXPENSES---- $ _____

TOTAL GIFT EXPENSES: $ _____

MONTHLY EXPENSES
HOUSING EXPENSES

RENTER'S / HOMEOWNER'S INSURANCE--- $ _____
CLEANING SUPPLIES------ $ _____
GARDENING SUPPLIES----- $ _____
FURNISHINGS---------- $ _____
LAUNDRY / DRY CLEANING- $ _____
HOME MAINTENANCE / REPAIRS-- $ _____
HOUSEHOLD NECESSITIES---- $ _____
OTHER HOUSING EXPENSES-- $ _____

TOTAL HOUSING EXPENSES: $ _____

RECREATION

VACATION(S)---------- $ _____
DINING OUT----------- $ _____
ENTERTAINMENT-------- $ _____
SOCIAL EVENTS-------- $ _____
OTHER RECREATION EXPENESES--- $ _____

TOTAL RECREATION EXPENSES: $ _____

SAVINGS

EMERGENCY FUND------------ $ _____
EDUCATION FUND------- $ _____
RETIREMENT FUND-------- $ _____

TOTAL SAVINGS: $ _____

MONTHLY EXPENSES

DEBTS

CREDIT CARD #1 --------------- $ _____
CREDIT CARD #2 --------------- $ _____
CREDIT CARD # 3 -------------- $ _____
CREDIT CARD # 4 -------------- $ _____
PRIVATE DEBTS --------------- $ _____
OTHER DEBTS ---------------- $ _____

TOTAL DEBTS : $ _____

OTHER EXPENSES

OTHER EXPENSE #1 ---------- $ _____
OTHER EXPENSE #2 ---------- $ _____
OTHER EXPENSE #3 ---------- $ _____

TOTAL OTHER EXPENSES : $ _____

MONTHLY BUDGET

TOTAL INCOME : $ _____
− TOTAL EXPENSES : $ _____
_____
MONEY REMAINING : $ _____

MONTHLY NOTES

February _____

MONTHLY BILL TRACKING

PAID	BILL NAME	DUE DATE	AMOUNT DUE	AMOUNT PAID	BALANCE	PAYMENT METHOD / NOTES
◯						
◯						
◯						
◯						
◯						
◯						
◯						
◯						
◯						
◯						
◯						
◯						
◯						
◯						
◯						
◯						
◯						
◯						
◯						
◯						
◯						
◯						
◯						
◯						
◯						
◯						
◯						

Create Your March Budget Here

MONTHLY INCOMES

#	SOURCE	AMOUNT	DATE
1.		$	
2.		$	
3.		$	
4.		$	
5.		$	

TOTAL INCOME: $_____

> *An investment in knowledge pays the best interest.*
> *-Benjamin Franklin*

MONTHLY EXPENSES
UTILITIES

RENT / MORTGAGE---------- $____
ELECTRICITY BILL---------- $____
WATER BILL---------- $____
SEWAGE / TRASH---------- $____
CABLE BILL---------- $____
INTERNET---------- $____
PHONE BILL(S)---------- $____

TOTAL UTILITIES: $_____

MONTHLY EXPENSES
HEALTHCARE

HEALTH INSURANCE---------- $____
LIFE INSURANCE---------- $____
DENTAL INSURANCE---------- $____
DOCTOR APPOINTMENT(S)- $____
DENTAL APPOINTMENT(S)- $____
OPTOMETRY APPOINTMENT(S)- $____
PERSCRIPTIONS---------- $____
OTHER MEDICAL EXPENSES--- $____

TOTAL HEALTHCARE: $_____

LIVING EXPENSES

GROCERIES---------- $____
BEAUTY SUPPLIES---------- $____
BEAUTY APPOINTMENTS---- $____
MEMBERSHIP DUES / FEES-- $____
DAYCARE / BABYSITTER ---- $____
School SUPPLIES---------- $____
SCHOOL CLUB(S) DUES /FEES-- $____
NEW CLOTHING---------- $____
ALLOWANCES---------- $____
OTHER LIVING EXPENSES---- $____

TOTAL LIVING EXPENSES: $_____

March _____

MONTHLY EXPENSES

PET EXPENSES

PET INSURANCE------------ $_____
PET FOOD------------------ $_____
VETERINARY APPOINTMENT(S)-- $_____
NEW TOYS / TREATS -------- $_____
PET SITTER / DAYCARE----- $_____
OTHER PET EXPENSES------ $_____

TOTAL PET EXPENSES: $_____

TRANSPORTATION

AUTOMOBILE INSURANCE----- $_____
AUTOMOBILE PAYMENTS---- $_____
MONTHLY FUEL COSTS------ $_____
REPAIRS / MAINTENANCE--- $_____
FARES / TICKETS / ETC.---- $_____
OTHER TRANSPORTATION EXPENSES-- $_____

TOTAL TRANSPORTATION: $_____

GIFT EXPENSES

MONTHLY BIRTHDAYS---------- $_____
MONTHLY HOLIDAYS------ $_____
OTHER GIFT EXPENSES------- $_____

TOTAL GIFT EXPENSES: $_____

MONTHLY EXPENSES

HOUSING EXPENSES

RENTER'S / HOMEOWNER'S INSURANCE--- $_____
CLEANING SUPPLIES------ $_____
GARDENING SUPPLIES------ $_____
FURNISHINGS---------- $_____
LAUNDRY / DRY CLEANING- $_____
HOME MAINTENANCE / REPAIRS-- $_____
HOUSEHOLD NECESSITIES---- $_____
OTHER HOUSING EXPENSES--- $_____

TOTAL HOUSING EXPENSES: $_____

RECREATION

VACATION(S)------------ $_____
DINING OUT----------- $_____
ENTERTAINMENT------- $_____
SOCIAL EVENTS-------- $_____
OTHER RECREATION EXPENESES--- $_____

TOTAL RECREATION EXPENSES: $_____

SAVINGS

EMERGENCY FUND----------- $_____
EDUCATION FUND------- $_____
RETIREMENT FUND-------- $_____

TOTAL SAVINGS: $_____

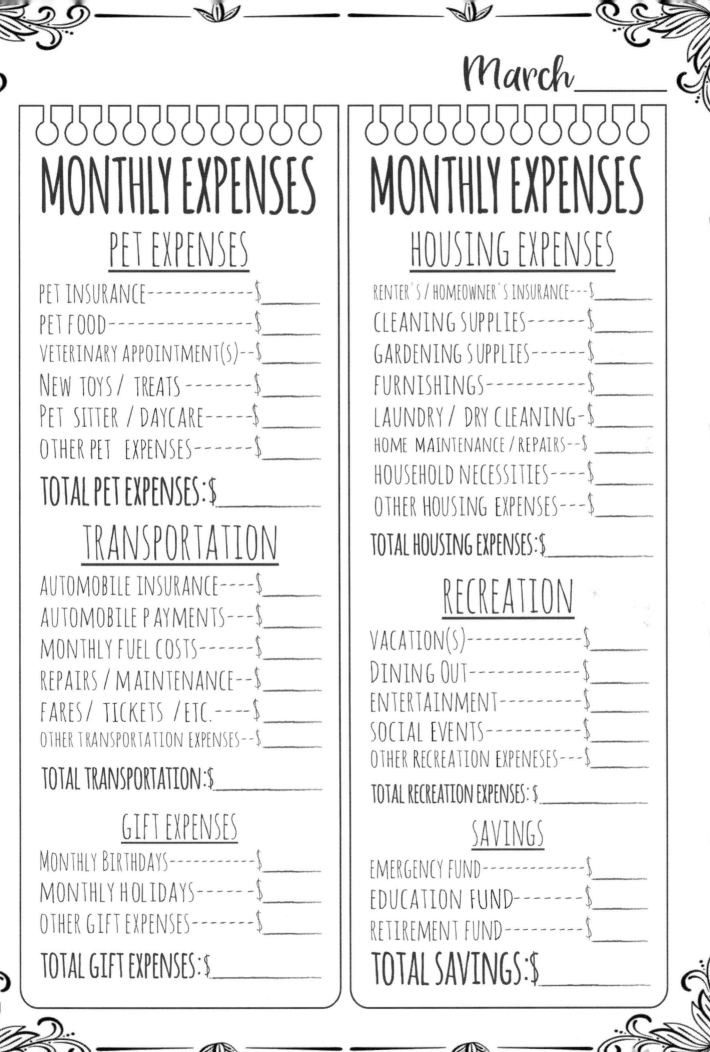

MONTHLY EXPENSES

DEBTS

CREDIT CARD #1 ----------- $_____
CREDIT CARD #2 ----------- $_____
CREDIT CARD # 3 ---------- $_____
CREDIT CARD #4 --------- $_____
PRIVATE DEBTS -------- $_____
OTHER DEBTS --------- $_____

TOTAL DEBTS: $_____

OTHER EXPENSES

OTHER EXPENSE #1 -------- $_____
OTHER EXPENSE #2 -------- $_____
OTHER EXPENSE #3 -------- $_____

TOTAL OTHER EXPENSES: $_____

MONTHLY BUDGET

TOTAL INCOME: $_____
– TOTAL EXPENSES: $_____

MONEY REMAINING: $_____

MONTHLY NOTES

March_____

MONTHLY BILL TRACKING

PAID	BILL NAME	DUE DATE	AMOUNT DUE	AMOUNT PAID	BALANCE	PAYMENT METHOD / NOTES
○						
○						
○						
○						
○						
○						
○						
○						
○						
○						
○						
○						
○						
○						
○						
○						
○						
○						
○						
○						
○						
○						
○						
○						

Create Your April Budget Here

MONTHLY INCOMES

#	SOURCE	AMOUNT	DATE
1.		$	
2.		$	
3.		$	
4.		$	
5.		$	

TOTAL INCOME: $ _____

Opportunity is missed by most people because it is dressed in overalls and looks like work.
—Thomas Edison

MONTHLY EXPENSES

UTILITIES

RENT / MORTGAGE --------- $ _____
ELECTRICITY BILL -------- $ _____
WATER BILL ------------- $ _____
SEWAGE / TRASH --------- $ _____
CABLE BILL ------------- $ _____
INTERNET -------------- $ _____
PHONE BILL(S) ---------- $ _____

TOTAL UTILITIES: $ _____

MONTHLY EXPENSES

HEALTHCARE

HEALTH INSURANCE --------- $ _____
LIFE INSURANCE ---------- $ _____
DENTAL INSURANCE -------- $ _____
DOCTOR APPOINTMENT(S) - $ _____
DENTAL APPOINTMENT(S) - $ _____
OPTOMETRY APPOINTMENT(S) - $ _____
PERSCRIPTIONS ---------- $ _____
OTHER MEDICAL EXPENSES --- $ _____

TOTAL HEALTHCARE: $ _____

LIVING EXPENSES

GROCERIES -------------- $ _____
BEAUTY SUPPLIES --------- $ _____
BEAUTY APPOINTMENTS ---- $ _____
MEMBERSHIP DUES / FEES -- $ _____
DAYCARE / BABYSITTER ---- $ _____
SCHOOL SUPPLIES --------- $ _____
SCHOOL CLUB(S) DUES / FEES -- $ _____
NEW CLOTHING ----------- $ _____
ALLOWANCES ------------ $ _____
OTHER LIVING EXPENSES ---- $ _____

TOTAL LIVING EXPENSES: $ _____

MONTHLY EXPENSES

PET EXPENSES

PET INSURANCE ------------- $ _____
PET FOOD ------------------ $ _____
VETERINARY APPOINTMENT(S) -- $ _____
New TOYS / TREATS --------- $ _____
Pet SITTER / DAYCARE ------ $ _____
OTHER PET EXPENSES -------- $ _____

TOTAL PET EXPENSES: $ _____

TRANSPORTATION

AUTOMOBILE INSURANCE ----- $ _____
AUTOMOBILE PAYMENTS ----- $ _____
MONTHLY FUEL COSTS ------- $ _____
REPAIRS / MAINTENANCE --- $ _____
FARES / TICKETS / ETC. ----- $ _____
OTHER TRANSPORTATION EXPENSES -- $ _____

TOTAL TRANSPORTATION: $ _____

GIFT EXPENSES

Monthly Birthdays ---------- $ _____
MONTHLY HOLIDAYS ------ $ _____
OTHER GIFT EXPENSES ------- $ _____

TOTAL GIFT EXPENSES: $ _____

MONTHLY EXPENSES

HOUSING EXPENSES

RENTER'S / HOMEOWNER'S INSURANCE --- $ _____
CLEANING SUPPLIES ------ $ _____
GARDENING SUPPLIES ------- $ _____
FURNISHINGS ----------- $ _____
LAUNDRY / DRY CLEANING - $ _____
HOME MAINTENANCE / REPAIRS -- $ _____
HOUSEHOLD NECESSITIES ---- $ _____
OTHER HOUSING EXPENSES --- $ _____

TOTAL HOUSING EXPENSES: $ _____

RECREATION

VACATION(S) ----------- $ _____
DINING OUT ----------- $ _____
ENTERTAINMENT --------- $ _____
SOCIAL EVENTS --------- $ _____
OTHER RECREATION EXPENSES --- $ _____

TOTAL RECREATION EXPENSES: $ _____

SAVINGS

EMERGENCY FUND ----------- $ _____
EDUCATION FUND --------- $ _____
RETIREMENT FUND ------- $ _____

TOTAL SAVINGS: $ _____

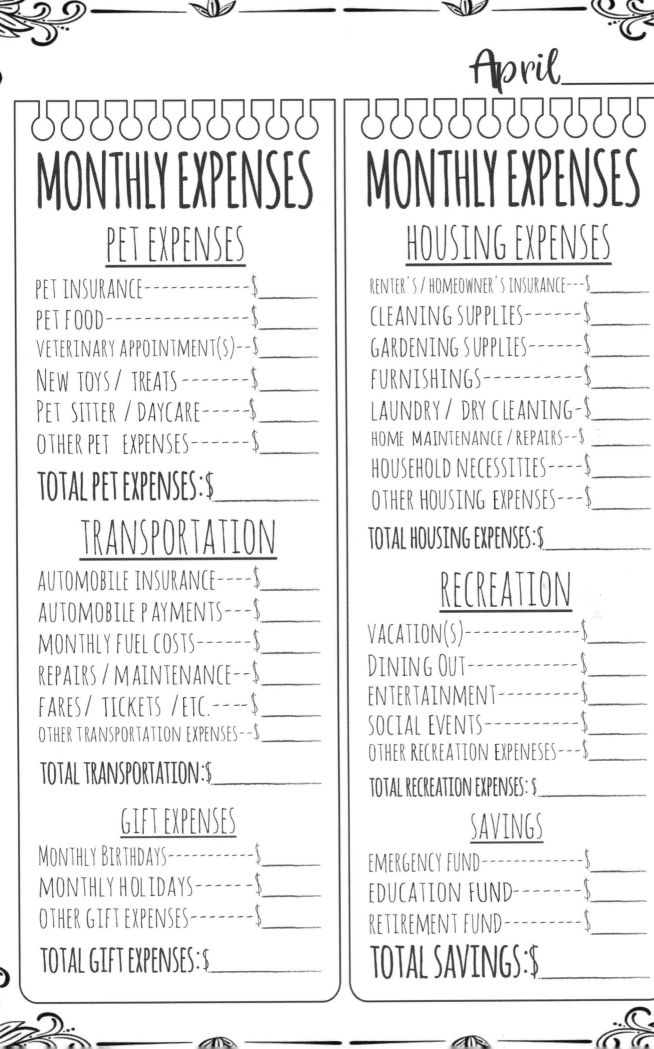

MONTHLY EXPENSES

DEBTS

CREDIT CARD #1----------$
CREDIT CARD #2----------$
CREDIT CARD #3----------$
CREDIT CARD #4----------$
PRIVATE DEBTS----------$
OTHER DEBTS----------$

TOTAL DEBTS: $_____

OTHER EXPENSES

OTHER EXPENSE #1--------$
OTHER EXPENSE #2--------$
OTHER EXPENSE #3--------$

TOTAL OTHER EXPENSES:$_____

MONTHLY BUDGET

TOTAL INCOME:$_____
− TOTAL EXPENSES:$_____

MONEY REMAINING:$_____

MONTHLY NOTES

April _____

MONTHLY BILL TRACKING

PAID	BILL NAME	DUE DATE	AMOUNT DUE	AMOUNT PAID	BALANCE	PAYMENT METHOD / NOTES
○						
○						
○						
○						
○						
○						
○						
○						
○						
○						
○						
○						
○						
○						
○						
○						
○						
○						
○						
○						
○						
○						
○						
○						

Create Your May Budget Here

MONTHLY INCOMES

#	SOURCE	AMOUNT	DATE
1.		$	
2.		$	
3.		$	
4.		$	
5.		$	

TOTAL INCOME: $ _____

> *It is not the man who has too little, but the man who craves more, that is poor.*
> *-Seneca*

MONTHLY EXPENSES
UTILITIES

RENT / MORTGAGE---------- $ _____
ELECTRICITY Bill---------- $ _____
WATER Bill---------- $ _____
SEWAGE / TRASH---------- $ _____
CABLE BILL---------- $ _____
INTERNET---------- $ _____
Phone Bill(S)---------- $ _____

TOTAL UTILITIES: $ _____

MONTHLY EXPENSES
HEALTHCARE

HEALTH INSURANCE---------- $ _____
Life Insurance---------- $ _____
DENTAL INSURANCE---------- $ _____
DOCTOR APPOINTMENT(S)-$ _____
DENTAL APPOINTMENT(S)-$ _____
OPTOMETRY APPOINTMENT(S)-$ _____
PERSCRIPTIONS---------- $ _____
OTHER MEDICAL EXPENSES--- $ _____

TOTAL HEALTHCARE: $ _____

LIVING EXPENSES

GROCERIES---------- $ _____
BEAUTY SUPPLIES---------- $ _____
BEAUTY APPOINTMENTS---- $ _____
MEMBERSHIP DUES / FEES-- $ _____
DAYCARE / BABYSITTER ---- $ _____
School SUPPLIES---------- $ _____
SCHOOL CLUB(S) DUES /FEES-- $ _____
NEW CLOTHING---------- $ _____
ALLOWANCES---------- $ _____
OTHER LIVING EEXPENSES---- $ _____

TOTAL LIVING EXPENSES: $ _____

May _____

MONTHLY EXPENSES

PET EXPENSES

PET INSURANCE----------- $_____
PET FOOD --------------- $_____
VETERINARY APPOINTMENT(S)-- $_____
NEW TOYS / TREATS ------- $_____
PET SITTER / DAYCARE----- $_____
OTHER PET EXPENSES------- $_____

TOTAL PET EXPENSES: $_____

TRANSPORTATION

AUTOMOBILE INSURANCE---- $_____
AUTOMOBILE PAYMENTS--- $_____
MONTHLY FUEL COSTS------- $_____
REPAIRS / MAINTENANCE-- $_____
FARES / TICKETS / ETC.---- $_____
OTHER TRANSPORTATION EXPENSES-- $_____

TOTAL TRANSPORTATION: $_____

GIFT EXPENSES

MONTHLY BIRTHDAYS---------- $_____
MONTHLY HOLIDAYS------ $_____
OTHER GIFT EXPENSES------- $_____

TOTAL GIFT EXPENSES: $_____

MONTHLY EXPENSES

HOUSING EXPENSES

RENTER'S / HOMEOWNER'S INSURANCE--- $_____
CLEANING SUPPLIES------ $_____
GARDENING SUPPLIES------ $_____
FURNISHINGS----------- $_____
LAUNDRY / DRY CLEANING- $_____
HOME MAINTENANCE / REPAIRS-- $_____
HOUSEHOLD NECESSITIES---- $_____
OTHER HOUSING EXPENSES--- $_____

TOTAL HOUSING EXPENSES: $_____

RECREATION

VACATION(S)------------- $_____
DINING OUT----------- $_____
ENTERTAINMENT-------- $_____
SOCIAL EVENTS--------- $_____
OTHER RECREATION EXPENSES--- $_____

TOTAL RECREATION EXPENSES: $_____

SAVINGS

EMERGENCY FUND----------- $_____
EDUCATION FUND------- $_____
RETIREMENT FUND--------- $_____

TOTAL SAVINGS: $_____

May _____

MONTHLY EXPENSES

DEBTS

CREDIT CARD #1 -------------- $ _____
CREDIT CARD #2 -------------- $ _____
CREDIT CARD # 3 ------------- $ _____
CREDIT CARD #4 ------------- $ _____
PRIVATE DEBTS ------------- $ _____
OTHER DEBTS ------------- $ _____

TOTAL DEBTS: $ _____

OTHER EXPENSES

OTHER EXPENSE #1 --------- $ _____
OTHER EXPENSE #2 --------- $ _____
OTHER EXPENSE #3 --------- $ _____

TOTAL OTHER EXPENSES: $ _____

MONTHLY BUDGET

TOTAL INCOME: $ _____
— TOTAL EXPENSES: $ _____
_____
MONEY REMAINING: $ _____

MONTHLY NOTES

_____
_____
_____
_____
_____
_____
_____
_____
_____
_____
_____
_____
_____
_____
_____
_____
_____
_____
_____
_____
_____
_____
_____
_____
_____
_____
_____
_____
_____
_____
_____
_____

MONTHLY BILL TRACKING

May _____

PAID	BILL NAME	DUE DATE	AMOUNT DUE	AMOUNT PAID	BALANCE	PAYMENT METHOD / NOTES
○						
○						
○						
○						
○						
○						
○						
○						
○						
○						
○						
○						
○						
○						
○						
○						
○						
○						
○						
○						
○						
○						
○						
○						
○						

Create Your June Budget Here

MONTHLY INCOMES

#	SOURCE	AMOUNT	DATE
1.		$	
2.		$	
3.		$	
4.		$	
5.		$	

TOTAL INCOME: $_____

> *Money is a terrible master but an excellent servant.*
> *—P.T. Barnum*

MONTHLY EXPENSES
UTILITIES

RENT / MORTGAGE----------$_____
ELECTRICITY BILL---------$_____
WATER BILL--------------$_____
SEWAGE / TRASH----------$_____
CABLE BILL-------------$_____
INTERNET-------------$_____
PHONE BILL(S)----------$_____

TOTAL UTILITIES: $_____

MONTHLY EXPENSES
HEALTHCARE

HEALTH INSURANCE----------$_____
LIFE INSURANCE----------$_____
DENTAL INSURANCE-------$_____
DOCTOR APPOINTMENT(S)-$_____
DENTAL APPOINTMENT(S)-$_____
OPTOMETRY APPOINTMENT(S)-$_____
PERSCRIPTIONS----------$_____
OTHER MEDICAL EXPENSES---$_____

TOTAL HEALTHCARE: $_____

LIVING EXPENSES

GROCERIES---------------$_____
BEAUTY SUPPLIES----------$_____
BEAUTY APPOINTMENTS----$_____
MEMBERSHIP DUES / FEES--$_____
DAYCARE / BABYSITTER----$_____
School SUPPLIES----------$_____
SCHOOL CLUB(S) DUES / FEES--$_____
NEW CLOTHING----------$_____
ALLOWANCES-----------$_____
OTHER LIVING EXPENSES----$_____

TOTAL LIVING EXPENSES: $_____

June _____

MONTHLY EXPENSES

PET EXPENSES

PET INSURANCE---------- $ _____
PET FOOD-------------- $ _____
VETERINARY APPOINTMENT(S)-- $ _____
New TOYS / TREATS------- $ _____
Pet SITTER / DAYCARE----- $ _____
OTHER PET EXPENSES------ $ _____

TOTAL PET EXPENSES: $ _____

TRANSPORTATION

AUTOMOBILE INSURANCE---- $ _____
AUTOMOBILE PAYMENTS--- $ _____
MONTHLY FUEL COSTS------ $ _____
REPAIRS / MAINTENANCE-- $ _____
FARES / TICKETS / ETC. ---- $ _____
OTHER TRANSPORTATION EXPENSES-- $ _____

TOTAL TRANSPORTATION: $ _____

GIFT EXPENSES

Monthly Birthdays--------- $ _____
MONTHLY HOLIDAYS----- $ _____
OTHER GIFT EXPENSES----- $ _____

TOTAL GIFT EXPENSES: $ _____

MONTHLY EXPENSES

HOUSING EXPENSES

RENTER'S / HOMEOWNER'S INSURANCE--- $ _____
CLEANING SUPPLIES------ $ _____
GARDENING SUPPLIES------ $ _____
FURNISHINGS---------- $ _____
LAUNDRY / DRY CLEANING- $ _____
HOME MAINTENANCE / REPAIRS-- $ _____
HOUSEHOLD NECESSITIES---- $ _____
OTHER HOUSING EXPENSES--- $ _____

TOTAL HOUSING EXPENSES: $ _____

RECREATION

VACATION(S)---------- $ _____
DINING OUT---------- $ _____
ENTERTAINMENT-------- $ _____
SOCIAL EVENTS-------- $ _____
OTHER RECREATION EXPENESES--- $ _____

TOTAL RECREATION EXPENSES: $ _____

SAVINGS

EMERGENCY FUND---------- $ _____
EDUCATION FUND------- $ _____
RETIREMENT FUND------- $ _____

TOTAL SAVINGS: $ _____

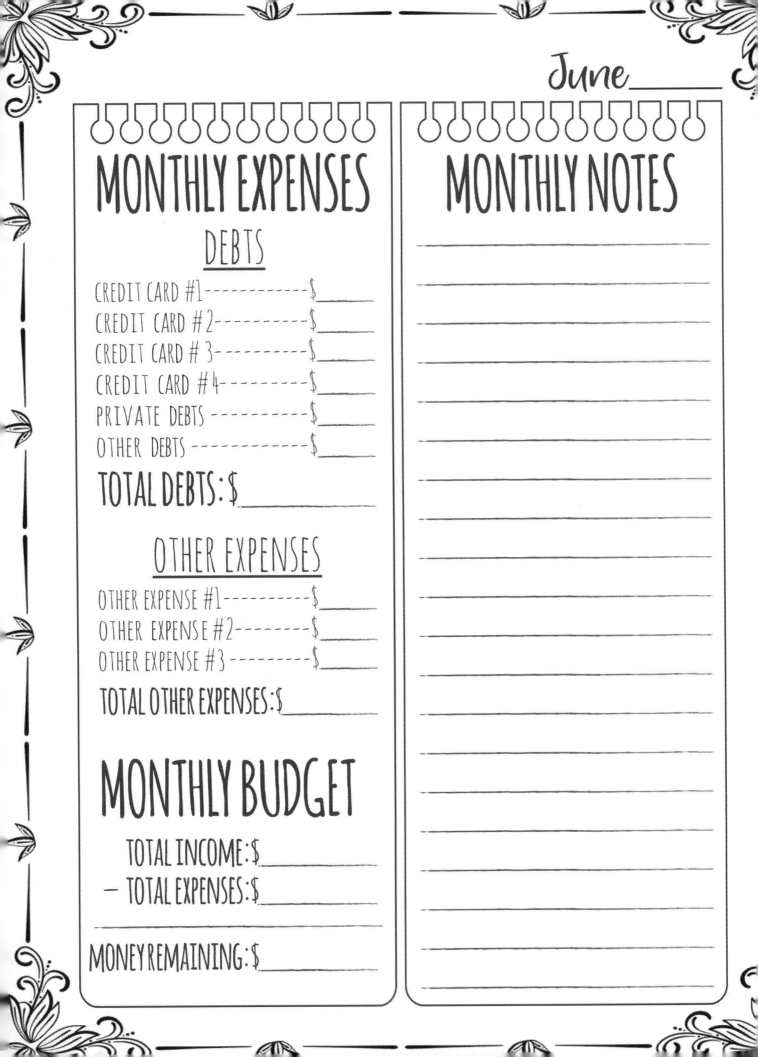

June _____

MONTHLY EXPENSES

DEBTS

CREDIT CARD #1 ----------- $ _____
CREDIT CARD #2 ----------- $ _____
CREDIT CARD # 3 ----------- $ _____
CREDIT CARD # 4 ----------- $ _____
PRIVATE DEBTS ----------- $ _____
OTHER DEBTS ----------- $ _____

TOTAL DEBTS: $ _____

OTHER EXPENSES

OTHER EXPENSE #1 ----------- $ _____
OTHER EXPENSE #2 ----------- $ _____
OTHER EXPENSE #3 ----------- $ _____

TOTAL OTHER EXPENSES: $ _____

MONTHLY BUDGET

TOTAL INCOME: $ _____
− TOTAL EXPENSES: $ _____

MONEY REMAINING: $ _____

MONTHLY NOTES

MONTHLY BILL TRACKING

June_____

PAID	BILL NAME	DUE DATE	AMOUNT DUE	AMOUNT PAID	BALANCE	PAYMENT METHOD / NOTES
○						
○						
○						
○						
○						
○						
○						
○						
○						
○						
○						
○						
○						
○						
○						
○						
○						
○						
○						
○						
○						
○						
○						
○						
○						
○						

Create Your July Budget Here

MONTHLY INCOMES

#	SOURCE	AMOUNT	DATE
1.		$	
2.		$	
3.		$	
4.		$	
5.		$	

TOTAL INCOME: $_____

> A journey of a thousand miles must begin with a single step.
> -Lao Tzu

MONTHLY EXPENSES
UTILITIES

RENT / MORTGAGE----------$_____
ELECTRICITY Bill----------$_____
WATER Bill----------$_____
SEWAGE / TRASH----------$_____
CABLE BILL----------$_____
INTERNET----------$_____
Phone Bill(s)----------$_____

TOTAL UTILITIES: $_____

MONTHLY EXPENSES
HEALTHCARE

HEALTH INSURANCE----------$_____
Life Insurance----------$_____
DENTAL INSURANCE----------$_____
DOCTOR APPOINTMENT(S)-$_____
DENTAL APPOINTMENT(S)-$_____
OPTOMETRY APPOINTMENT(S)-$_____
PERSCRIPTIONS----------$_____
OTHER MEDICAL EXPENSES---$_____

TOTAL HEALTHCARE: $_____

LIVING EXPENSES

GROCERIES----------$_____
BEAUTY SUPPLIES----------$_____
BEAUTY APPOINTMENTS----$_____
MEMBERSHIP DUES / FEES--$_____
DAYCARE / BABYSITTER----$_____
School SUPPLIES----------$_____
SCHOOL CLUB(S) DUES / FEES--$_____
NEW CLOTHING----------$_____
ALLOWANCES----------$_____
OTHER LIVING EXPENSES----$_____

TOTAL LIVING EXPENSES: $_____

MONTHLY EXPENSES

PET EXPENSES

PET INSURANCE---------------- $ _____
PET FOOD--------------------- $ _____
VETERINARY APPOINTMENT(S)-- $ _____
NEW TOYS / TREATS -------- $ _____
PET SITTER / DAYCARE----- $ _____
OTHER PET EXPENSES------ $ _____

TOTAL PET EXPENSES: $ _____

TRANSPORTATION

AUTOMOBILE INSURANCE---- $ _____
AUTOMOBILE PAYMENTS--- $ _____
MONTHLY FUEL COSTS------ $ _____
REPAIRS / MAINTENANCE-- $ _____
FARES / TICKETS / ETC.---- $ _____
OTHER TRANSPORTATION EXPENSES-- $ _____

TOTAL TRANSPORTATION: $ _____

GIFT EXPENSES

MONTHLY BIRTHDAYS--------- $ _____
MONTHLY HOLIDAYS------ $ _____
OTHER GIFT EXPENSES--- $ _____

TOTAL GIFT EXPENSES: $ _____

MONTHLY EXPENSES

HOUSING EXPENSES

RENTER'S / HOMEOWNER'S INSURANCE--- $ _____
CLEANING SUPPLIES------ $ _____
GARDENING SUPPLIES------ $ _____
FURNISHINGS----------- $ _____
LAUNDRY / DRY CLEANING- $ _____
HOME MAINTENANCE / REPAIRS-- $ _____
HOUSEHOLD NECESSITIES---- $ _____
OTHER HOUSING EXPENSES--- $ _____

TOTAL HOUSING EXPENSES: $ _____

RECREATION

VACATION(S)----------- $ _____
DINING OUT----------- $ _____
ENTERTAINMENT-------- $ _____
SOCIAL EVENTS-------- $ _____
OTHER RECREATION EXPENESES--- $ _____

TOTAL RECREATION EXPENSES: $ _____

SAVINGS

EMERGENCY FUND------------ $ _____
EDUCATION FUND------ $ _____
RETIREMENT FUND-------- $ _____

TOTAL SAVINGS: $ _____

MONTHLY EXPENSES

DEBTS

CREDIT CARD #1 ----------- $ _____
CREDIT CARD #2 ----------- $ _____
CREDIT CARD #3 ----------- $ _____
CREDIT CARD #4 ----------- $ _____
PRIVATE DEBTS ----------- $ _____
OTHER DEBTS ----------- $ _____

TOTAL DEBTS: $ _____

OTHER EXPENSES

OTHER EXPENSE #1 --------- $ _____
OTHER EXPENSE #2 --------- $ _____
OTHER EXPENSE #3 --------- $ _____

TOTAL OTHER EXPENSES: $ _____

MONTHLY BUDGET

TOTAL INCOME: $ _____
− TOTAL EXPENSES: $ _____
_____
MONEY REMAINING: $ _____

MONTHLY NOTES

_____
_____
_____
_____
_____
_____
_____
_____
_____
_____
_____
_____
_____
_____
_____
_____
_____
_____
_____
_____
_____
_____
_____
_____
_____
_____
_____
_____

MONTHLY BILL TRACKING

July _____

PAID	BILL NAME	DUE DATE	AMOUNT DUE	AMOUNT PAID	BALANCE	PAYMENT METHOD / NOTES
○						
○						
○						
○						
○						
○						
○						
○						
○						
○						
○						
○						
○						
○						
○						
○						
○						
○						
○						
○						
○						
○						
○						
○						
○						
○						

Create Your August Budget Here

MONTHLY INCOMES

#	SOURCE	AMOUNT	DATE
1.		$	
2.		$	
3.		$	
4.		$	
5.		$	

TOTAL INCOME: $ _____

Fortune sides with him who dares.
-Virgil

MONTHLY EXPENSES
UTILITIES

RENT / MORTGAGE————————$_____
ELECTRICITY Bill————————$_____
WATER Bill————————————$_____
SEWAGE / TRASH————————$_____
CABLE BILL————————————$_____
INTERNET————————————————$_____
Phone Bill(s)————————————$_____

TOTAL UTILITIES: $ _____

MONTHLY EXPENSES
HEALTHCARE

HEALTH INSURANCE————————$_____
Life Insurance————————————$_____
DENTAL INSURANCE————————$_____
DOCTOR APPOINTMENT(S)—$_____
DENTAL APPOINTMENT(S)—$_____
OPTOMETRY APPOINTMENT(S)—$_____
PERSCRIPTIONS————————————$_____
OTHER MEDICAL EXPENSES———$_____

TOTAL HEALTHCARE: $ _____

LIVING EXPENSES

GROCERIES————————————————$_____
BEAUTY SUPPLIES————————$_____
BEAUTY APPOINTMENTS————$_____
MEMBERSHIP DUES / FEES——$_____
DAYCARE / BABYSITTER————$_____
School SUPPLIES————————————$_____
SCHOOL CLUB(S) DUES / FEES——$_____
NEW CLOTHING————————————$_____
ALLOWANCES————————————————$_____
OTHER LIVING EXPENSES————$_____

TOTAL LIVING EXPENSES: $ _____

MONTHLY EXPENSES

PET EXPENSES

PET INSURANCE----------- $____
PET FOOD---------------- $____
VETERINARY APPOINTMENT(S)-- $____
New toys / TREATS ------- $____
Pet SITTER / DAYCARE----- $____
OTHER PET EXPENSES------- $____

TOTAL PET EXPENSES: $____

TRANSPORTATION

AUTOMOBILE INSURANCE---- $____
AUTOMOBILE PAYMENTS--- $____
MONTHLY FUEL COSTS------ $____
REPAIRS / MAINTENANCE-- $____
FARES / TICKETS / ETC. ---- $____
OTHER TRANSPORTATION EXPENSES-- $____

TOTAL TRANSPORTATION: $____

GIFT EXPENSES

Monthly Birthdays-------- $____
MONTHLY HOLIDAYS------ $____
OTHER GIFT EXPENSES------ $____

TOTAL GIFT EXPENSES: $____

MONTHLY EXPENSES

HOUSING EXPENSES

RENTER'S / HOMEOWNER'S INSURANCE--- $____
CLEANING SUPPLIES------ $____
GARDENING SUPPLIES------ $____
FURNISHINGS----------- $____
LAUNDRY / DRY CLEANING-$____
HOME MAINTENANCE / REPAIRS-- $____
HOUSEHOLD NECESSITIES---- $____
OTHER HOUSING EXPENSES--- $____

TOTAL HOUSING EXPENSES: $____

RECREATION

VACATION(S)------------- $____
DINING OUT------------- $____
ENTERTAINMENT--------- $____
SOCIAL EVENTS--------- $____
OTHER RECREATION EXPENESES--- $____

TOTAL RECREATION EXPENSES: $____

SAVINGS

EMERGENCY FUND---------- $____
EDUCATION FUND------- $____
RETIREMENT FUND--------- $____

TOTAL SAVINGS: $____

MONTHLY EXPENSES

DEBTS

CREDIT CARD #1 ----------- $ _____
CREDIT CARD #2 ----------- $ _____
CREDIT CARD #3 ----------- $ _____
CREDIT CARD #4 ----------- $ _____
PRIVATE DEBTS ----------- $ _____
OTHER DEBTS ----------- $ _____

TOTAL DEBTS: $ _____

OTHER EXPENSES

OTHER EXPENSE #1 --------- $ _____
OTHER EXPENSE #2 --------- $ _____
OTHER EXPENSE #3 --------- $ _____

TOTAL OTHER EXPENSES: $ _____

MONTHLY BUDGET

TOTAL INCOME: $ _____
– TOTAL EXPENSES: $ _____
_____
MONEY REMAINING: $ _____

MONTHLY NOTES

August

MONTHLY BILL TRACKING

PAID	BILL NAME	DUE DATE	AMOUNT DUE	AMOUNT PAID	BALANCE	PAYMENT METHOD / NOTES
◯						
◯						
◯						
◯						
◯						
◯						
◯						
◯						
◯						
◯						
◯						
◯						
◯						
◯						
◯						
◯						
◯						
◯						
◯						
◯						
◯						
◯						
◯						
◯						
◯						

Create Your September Budget Here

MONTHLY INCOMES

#	SOURCE	AMOUNT	DATE
1.		$	
2.		$	
3.		$	
4.		$	
5.		$	

TOTAL INCOME: $_____

No wealth can ever make a bad man at peace with himself.
-Plato

MONTHLY EXPENSES
UTILITIES

RENT / MORTGAGE---------- $_____
ELECTRICITY Bill---------- $_____
WATER Bill---------- $_____
SEWAGE / TRASH---------- $_____
CABLE BILL---------- $_____
INTERNET---------- $_____
Phone Bill(s)---------- $_____

TOTAL UTILITIES: $_____

MONTHLY EXPENSES
HEALTHCARE

HEALTH INSURANCE---------- $_____
LIFE INSURANCE---------- $_____
DENTAL INSURANCE------- $_____
DOCTOR APPOINTMENT(S)-$_____
DENTAL APPOINTMENT(S)-$_____
OPTOMETRY APPOINTMENT(S)-$_____
PERSCRIPTIONS---------- $_____
OTHER MEDICAL EXPENSES---$_____

TOTAL HEALTHCARE: $_____

LIVING EXPENSES

GROCERIES---------- $_____
BEAUTY SUPPLIES---------- $_____
BEAUTY APPOINTMENTS---- $_____
MEMBERSHIP DUES / FEES--$_____
DAYCARE / BABYSITTER ---- $_____
School SUPPLIES---------- $_____
SCHOOL CLUB(S) DUES /FEES--$_____
NEW CLOTHING---------- $_____
ALLOWANCES---------- $_____
OTHER LIVING EXPENSES---- $_____

TOTAL LIVING EXPENSES: $_____

MONTHLY EXPENSES

PET EXPENSES

PET INSURANCE————————— $ _____
PET FOOD————————————— $ _____
VETERINARY APPOINTMENT(S)—— $ _____
NEW TOYS / TREATS ————— $ _____
PET SITTER / DAYCARE———— $ _____
OTHER PET EXPENSES—————— $ _____

TOTAL PET EXPENSES: $ _____

TRANSPORTATION

AUTOMOBILE INSURANCE———— $ _____
AUTOMOBILE PAYMENTS——— $ _____
MONTHLY FUEL COSTS——————— $ _____
REPAIRS / MAINTENANCE—— $ _____
FARES / TICKETS / ETC.———— $ _____
OTHER TRANSPORTATION EXPENSES—— $ _____

TOTAL TRANSPORTATION: $ _____

GIFT EXPENSES

MONTHLY BIRTHDAYS————————— $ _____
MONTHLY HOLIDAYS——————— $ _____
OTHER GIFT EXPENSES———————— $ _____

TOTAL GIFT EXPENSES: $ _____

MONTHLY EXPENSES

HOUSING EXPENSES

RENTER'S / HOMEOWNER'S INSURANCE——— $ _____
CLEANING SUPPLIES——————— $ _____
GARDENING SUPPLIES—————— $ _____
FURNISHINGS————————————— $ _____
LAUNDRY / DRY CLEANING— $ _____
HOME MAINTENANCE / REPAIRS—— $ _____
HOUSEHOLD NECESSITIES———— $ _____
OTHER HOUSING EXPENSES——— $ _____

TOTAL HOUSING EXPENSES: $ _____

RECREATION

VACATION(S)——————————— $ _____
DINING OUT———————————— $ _____
ENTERTAINMENT———————— $ _____
SOCIAL EVENTS————————— $ _____
OTHER RECREATION EXPENESES——— $ _____

TOTAL RECREATION EXPENSES: $ _____

SAVINGS

EMERGENCY FUND——————— $ _____
EDUCATION FUND———————— $ _____
RETIREMENT FUND—————— $ _____

TOTAL SAVINGS: $ _____

MONTHLY EXPENSES

DEBTS

CREDIT CARD #1----------- $____
CREDIT CARD #2----------- $____
CREDIT CARD # 3----------- $____
CREDIT CARD #4--------- $____
PRIVATE DEBTS --------- $____
OTHER DEBTS ---------- $____

TOTAL DEBTS: $_____

OTHER EXPENSES

OTHER EXPENSE #1--------- $____
OTHER EXPENSE #2--------- $____
OTHER EXPENSE #3--------- $____

TOTAL OTHER EXPENSES: $_____

MONTHLY BUDGET

TOTAL INCOME: $_____
− TOTAL EXPENSES: $_____
_____
MONEY REMAINING: $_____

MONTHLY NOTES

September _____

MONTHLY BILL TRACKING

PAID	BILL NAME	DUE DATE	AMOUNT DUE	AMOUNT PAID	BALANCE	PAYMENT METHOD / NOTES
○						
○						
○						
○						
○						
○						
○						
○						
○						
○						
○						
○						
○						
○						
○						
○						
○						
○						
○						
○						
○						
○						
○						
○						
○						
○						
○						

Create Your October Budget Here

MONTHLY INCOMES

#	SOURCE	AMOUNT	DATE
1.		$	
2.		$	
3.		$	
4.		$	
5.		$	

TOTAL INCOME: $ _____

Do not go where the path may lead, go instead where there is no path and leave a trail.
-Ralph Waldo Emerson

MONTHLY EXPENSES
UTILITIES

RENT / MORTGAGE --------- $ _____
ELECTRICITY Bill --------- $ _____
WATER Bill --------- $ _____
SEWAGE / TRASH --------- $ _____
CABLE BILL --------- $ _____
INTERNET --------- $ _____
Phone Bill(s) --------- $ _____

TOTAL UTILITIES: $ _____

MONTHLY EXPENSES
HEALTHCARE

HEALTH INSURANCE --------- $ _____
LIFE INSURANCE --------- $ _____
DENTAL INSURANCE ------- $ _____
DOCTOR APPOINTMENT(S) - $ _____
DENTAL APPOINTMENT(S) - $ _____
OPTOMETRY APPOINTMENT(S) - $ _____
PERSCRIPTIONS --------- $ _____
OTHER MEDICAL EXPENSES --- $ _____

TOTAL HEALTHCARE: $ _____

LIVING EXPENSES

GROCERIES --------- $ _____
BEAUTY SUPPLIES --------- $ _____
BEAUTY APPOINTMENTS ---- $ _____
MEMBERSHIP DUES / FEES -- $ _____
DAYCARE / BABYSITTER ---- $ _____
School SUPPLIES --------- $ _____
SCHOOL CLUB(S) DUES / FEES -- $ _____
NEW CLOTHING --------- $ _____
ALLOWANCES --------- $ _____
OTHER LIVING EXPENSES ---- $ _____

TOTAL LIVING EXPENSES: $ _____

MONTHLY EXPENSES

PET EXPENSES

PET INSURANCE------------ $_____
PET FOOD---------------- $_____
VETERINARY APPOINTMENT(S)-- $_____
NEW TOYS / TREATS ------- $_____
PET SITTER / DAYCARE----- $_____
OTHER PET EXPENSES------ $_____

TOTAL PET EXPENSES: $_____

TRANSPORTATION

AUTOMOBILE INSURANCE---- $_____
AUTOMOBILE PAYMENTS--- $_____
MONTHLY FUEL COSTS------ $_____
REPAIRS / MAINTENANCE-- $_____
FARES / TICKETS / ETC. ---- $_____
OTHER TRANSPORTATION EXPENSES-- $_____

TOTAL TRANSPORTATION: $_____

GIFT EXPENSES

MONTHLY BIRTHDAYS--------- $_____
MONTHLY HOLIDAYS------ $_____
OTHER GIFT EXPENSES------- $_____

TOTAL GIFT EXPENSES: $_____

MONTHLY EXPENSES

HOUSING EXPENSES

RENTER'S / HOMEOWNER'S INSURANCE---$_____
CLEANING SUPPLIES------- $_____
GARDENING SUPPLIES------- $_____
FURNISHINGS------------ $_____
LAUNDRY / DRY CLEANING- $_____
HOME MAINTENANCE / REPAIRS--$_____
HOUSEHOLD NECESSITIES---- $_____
OTHER HOUSING EXPENSES---$_____

TOTAL HOUSING EXPENSES: $_____

RECREATION

VACATION(S)------------- $_____
DINING OUT------------- $_____
ENTERTAINMENT--------- $_____
SOCIAL EVENTS--------- $_____
OTHER RECREATION EXPENESES---$_____

TOTAL RECREATION EXPENSES: $_____

SAVINGS

EMERGENCY FUND------------ $_____
EDUCATION FUND------- $_____
RETIREMENT FUND------- $_____

TOTAL SAVINGS: $_____

October _____

MONTHLY EXPENSES

DEBTS

CREDIT CARD #1 ------------- $ _____
CREDIT CARD #2 ------------- $ _____
CREDIT CARD # 3 ------------ $ _____
CREDIT CARD #4 ------------- $ _____
PRIVATE DEBTS ------------- $ _____
OTHER DEBTS ------------- $ _____

TOTAL DEBTS: $ _____

OTHER EXPENSES

OTHER EXPENSE #1 ---------- $ _____
OTHER EXPENSE #2 ---------- $ _____
OTHER EXPENSE #3 ---------- $ _____

TOTAL OTHER EXPENSES: $ _____

MONTHLY BUDGET

TOTAL INCOME: $ _____
— TOTAL EXPENSES: $ _____

MONEY REMAINING: $ _____

MONTHLY NOTES

_____
_____
_____
_____
_____
_____
_____
_____
_____
_____
_____
_____
_____
_____
_____
_____
_____
_____
_____
_____
_____
_____
_____
_____
_____
_____
_____
_____
_____
_____

October_____

MONTHLY BILL TRACKING

PAID	BILL NAME	DUE DATE	AMOUNT DUE	AMOUNT PAID	BALANCE	PAYMENT METHOD / NOTES
○						
○						
○						
○						
○						
○						
○						
○						
○						
○						
○						
○						
○						
○						
○						
○						
○						
○						
○						
○						
○						
○						
○						
○						
○						
○						
○						
○						

Create Your November Budget Here

MONTHLY INCOMES

#	SOURCE	AMOUNT	DATE
1.		$	
2.		$	
3.		$	
4.		$	
5.		$	

TOTAL INCOME: $_____

> *Let no feeling of discouragement prey upon you, and in the end you are sure to succeed.*
> *-Abraham Lincoln*

MONTHLY EXPENSES
UTILITIES

RENT / MORTGAGE----------$____

ELECTRICITY BILL----------$____

WATER BILL-------------$____

SEWAGE / TRASH---------$____

CABLE BILL------------$____

INTERNET-------------$____

Phone BILL(S)----------$____

TOTAL UTILITIES: $_____

MONTHLY EXPENSES
HEALTHCARE

HEALTH INSURANCE----------$____

LIFE INSURANCE----------$____

DENTAL INSURANCE--------$____

DOCTOR APPOINTMENT(S)-$____

DENTAL APPOINTMENT(S)-$____

OPTOMETRY APPOINTMENT(S)-$____

PERSCRIPTIONS----------$____

OTHER MEDICAL EXPENSES---$____

TOTAL HEALTHCARE: $_____

LIVING EXPENSES

GROCERIES---------------$____

BEAUTY SUPPLIES---------$____

BEAUTY APPOINTMENTS----$____

MEMBERSHIP DUES / FEES--$____

DAYCARE / BABYSITTER----$____

School SUPPLIES----------$____

SCHOOL CLUB(S) DUES / FEES--$____

NEW CLOTHING----------$____

ALLOWANCES-----------$____

OTHER LIVING EXPENSES----$____

TOTAL LIVING EXPENSES: $_____

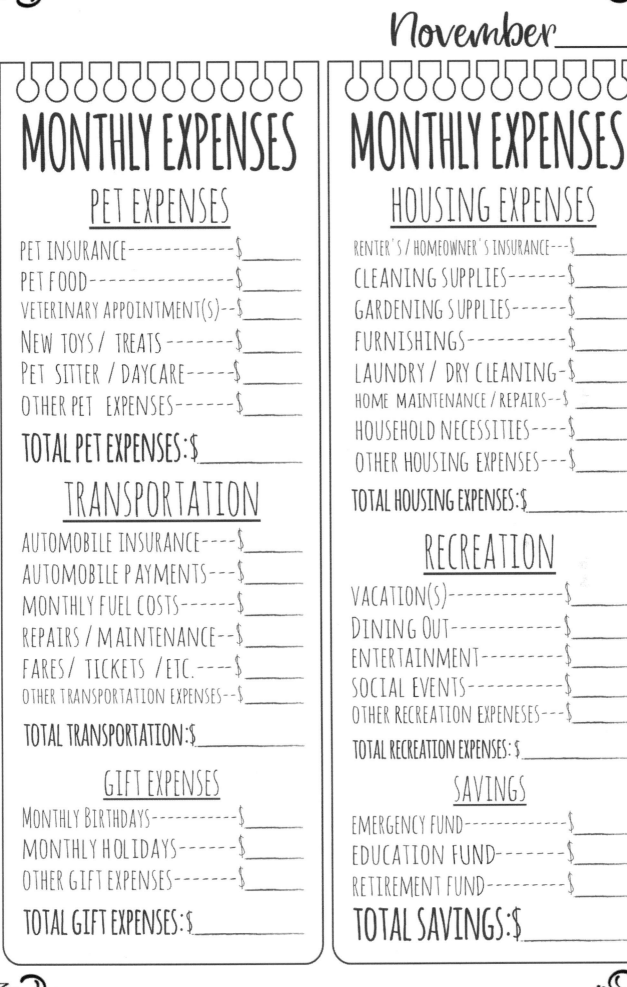

MONTHLY EXPENSES

PET EXPENSES

PET INSURANCE---------- $_____
PET FOOD------------- $_____
VETERINARY APPOINTMENT(S)-- $_____
New toys / TREATS ------ $_____
Pet sitter / daycare----- $_____
OTHER PET EXPENSES------ $_____

TOTAL PET EXPENSES: $_____

TRANSPORTATION

AUTOMOBILE INSURANCE---- $_____
AUTOMOBILE PAYMENTS--- $_____
MONTHLY FUEL COSTS------ $_____
REPAIRS / MAINTENANCE-- $_____
FARES / TICKETS / ETC.---- $_____
OTHER TRANSPORTATION EXPENSES-- $_____

TOTAL TRANSPORTATION: $_____

GIFT EXPENSES

Monthly Birthdays--------- $_____
MONTHLY HOLIDAYS----- $_____
OTHER GIFT EXPENSES------ $_____

TOTAL GIFT EXPENSES: $_____

MONTHLY EXPENSES

HOUSING EXPENSES

RENTER'S / HOMEOWNER'S INSURANCE--- $_____
CLEANING SUPPLIES------- $_____
GARDENING SUPPLIES------ $_____
FURNISHINGS---------- $_____
LAUNDRY / DRY CLEANING- $_____
HOME MAINTENANCE / REPAIRS-- $_____
HOUSEHOLD NECESSITIES---- $_____
OTHER HOUSING EXPENSES--- $_____

TOTAL HOUSING EXPENSES: $_____

RECREATION

VACATION(S)---------- $_____
DINING OUT---------- $_____
ENTERTAINMENT--------- $_____
SOCIAL EVENTS--------- $_____
OTHER RECREATION EXPENESES--- $_____

TOTAL RECREATION EXPENSES: $_____

SAVINGS

EMERGENCY FUND---------- $_____
EDUCATION FUND------- $_____
RETIREMENT FUND-------- $_____

TOTAL SAVINGS: $_____

MONTHLY EXPENSES

DEBTS

CREDIT CARD #1 ----------- $ _____
CREDIT CARD #2 ----------- $ _____
CREDIT CARD # 3 ----------- $ _____
CREDIT CARD #4 ----------- $ _____
PRIVATE DEBTS ----------- $ _____
OTHER DEBTS ----------- $ _____

TOTAL DEBTS: $ _____

OTHER EXPENSES

OTHER EXPENSE #1 ---------- $ _____
OTHER EXPENSE #2 ---------- $ _____
OTHER EXPENSE #3 ---------- $ _____

TOTAL OTHER EXPENSES: $ _____

MONTHLY BUDGET

TOTAL INCOME: $ _____
− TOTAL EXPENSES: $ _____
_____
MONEY REMAINING: $ _____

MONTHLY NOTES

_____
_____
_____
_____
_____
_____
_____
_____
_____
_____
_____
_____
_____
_____
_____
_____
_____
_____
_____
_____
_____
_____
_____
_____
_____
_____
_____
_____

November

MONTHLY BILL TRACKING

PAID	BILL NAME	DUE DATE	AMOUNT DUE	AMOUNT PAID	BALANCE	PAYMENT METHOD / NOTES
○						
○						
○						
○						
○						
○						
○						
○						
○						
○						
○						
○						
○						
○						
○						
○						
○						
○						
○						
○						
○						
○						
○						
○						
○						

Create Your December Budget Here

MONTHLY INCOMES

#	SOURCE	AMOUNT	DATE
1.		$	
2.		$	
3.		$	
4.		$	
5.		$	

TOTAL INCOME: $_____

> Live as if you were to die tomorrow.
> Learn as if you were to live forever.
> -Mahatma Gandhi

MONTHLY EXPENSES
UTILITIES

RENT / MORTGAGE---------- $_____
ELECTRICITY BILL---------- $_____
WATER BILL---------- $_____
SEWAGE / TRASH---------- $_____
CABLE BILL---------- $_____
INTERNET---------- $_____
Phone Bill(s)---------- $_____

TOTAL UTILITIES: $_____

MONTHLY EXPENSES
HEALTHCARE

HEALTH INSURANCE---------- $_____
LIFE INSURANCE---------- $_____
DENTAL INSURANCE-------- $_____
DOCTOR APPOINTMENT(S)-$_____
DENTAL APPOINTMENT(S)-$_____
OPTOMETRY APPOINTMENT(S)-$_____
PERSCRIPTIONS---------- $_____
OTHER MEDICAL EXPENSES---$_____

TOTAL HEALTHCARE: $_____

LIVING EXPENSES

GROCERIES---------- $_____
BEAUTY SUPPLIES---------- $_____
BEAUTY APPOINTMENTS---- $_____
MEMBERSHIP DUES / FEES--$_____
DAYCARE / BABYSITTER ---- $_____
School SUPPLIES---------- $_____
SCHOOL CLUB(S) DUES / FEES--$_____
NEW CLOTHING---------- $_____
ALLOWANCES---------- $_____
OTHER LIVING EXPENSES----$_____

TOTAL LIVING EXPENSES: $_____

MONTHLY EXPENSES

PET EXPENSES

PET INSURANCE------------ $____
PET FOOD---------------- $____
VETERINARY APPOINTMENT(S)-- $____
NEW TOYS / TREATS ------- $____
PET SITTER / DAYCARE----- $____
OTHER PET EXPENSES------ $____

TOTAL PET EXPENSES: $____

TRANSPORTATION

AUTOMOBILE INSURANCE---- $____
AUTOMOBILE PAYMENTS--- $____
MONTHLY FUEL COSTS------ $____
REPAIRS / MAINTENANCE-- $____
FARES / TICKETS / ETC.---- $____
OTHER TRANSPORTATION EXPENSES-- $____

TOTAL TRANSPORTATION: $____

GIFT EXPENSES

MONTHLY BIRTHDAYS---------- $____
MONTHLY HOLIDAYS------- $____
OTHER GIFT EXPENSES---- $____

TOTAL GIFT EXPENSES: $____

MONTHLY EXPENSES

HOUSING EXPENSES

RENTER'S / HOMEOWNER'S INSURANCE--- $____
CLEANING SUPPLIES------ $____
GARDENING SUPPLIES------ $____
FURNISHINGS---------- $____
LAUNDRY / DRY CLEANING- $____
HOME MAINTENANCE / REPAIRS-- $____
HOUSEHOLD NECESSITIES---- $____
OTHER HOUSING EXPENSES--- $____

TOTAL HOUSING EXPENSES: $____

RECREATION

VACATION(S)---------- $____
DINING OUT----------- $____
ENTERTAINMENT------- $____
SOCIAL EVENTS-------- $____
OTHER RECREATION EXPENESES--- $____

TOTAL RECREATION EXPENSES: $____

SAVINGS

EMERGENCY FUND---------- $____
EDUCATION FUND------- $____
RETIREMENT FUND-------- $____

TOTAL SAVINGS: $____

December _____

MONTHLY EXPENSES

DEBTS

CREDIT CARD #1 --------- $ _____
CREDIT CARD #2 --------- $ _____
CREDIT CARD #3 --------- $ _____
CREDIT CARD #4 --------- $ _____
PRIVATE DEBTS --------- $ _____
OTHER DEBTS --------- $ _____

TOTAL DEBTS: $ _____

OTHER EXPENSES

OTHER EXPENSE #1 --------- $ _____
OTHER EXPENSE #2 --------- $ _____
OTHER EXPENSE #3 --------- $ _____

TOTAL OTHER EXPENSES: $ _____

MONTHLY BUDGET

TOTAL INCOME: $ _____
− TOTAL EXPENSES: $ _____
_____
MONEY REMAINING: $ _____

MONTHLY NOTES

_____
_____
_____
_____
_____
_____
_____
_____
_____
_____
_____
_____
_____
_____
_____
_____
_____
_____
_____
_____
_____
_____
_____
_____
_____
_____
_____
_____
_____
_____
_____

December

MONTHLY BILL TRACKING

PAID	BILL NAME	DUE DATE	AMOUNT DUE	AMOUNT PAID	BALANCE	PAYMENT METHOD / NOTES
○						
○						
○						
○						
○						
○						
○						
○						
○						
○						
○						
○						
○						
○						
○						
○						
○						
○						
○						
○						
○						
○						
○						
○						
○						
○						
○						

Made in the USA
Columbia, SC
03 September 2022

66593524R00057